COLLABORATION IN ORGANIZATIONS

*Alternatives to
Hierarchy*

William A. Kraus, Ph.D.

 **HUMAN SCIENCES PRESS**

72 Fifth Avenue   3 Henrietta Street
NEW YORK, NY 10011 ● LONDON, WC2E 8LU

Printed in the United States of America
0123456789   987654321

Library of Congress Cataloging in Publication Data

Kraus, William A
   Collaboration in organizations.

   Bibliography: p. 251
   Includes index.
   1. Organization.   2. Competition (Psychology)
I. Title.
HD31.K69   302.3′5   LC 80-11291
ISBN 0-87705-491-6

PERMISSIONS

Permission from the publishers to reproduce excerpts from the following selections is gratefully acknowledged.

Locke, E. A. "Toward a theory of task motivation and incentives," *Organizational Behavior and Human Performance*, 1968, *3*, pp. 179–180.

Hellriegel, D., and Slocum, J. W. *Management: A contingency approach* (Figures 14.2 and 14.4). © 1974, Addison-Wesley, Reading, Mass. Reprinted with permission.

Copyright © 1977 by Brothers Gibb B. V.
    Published in the U.S.A. by Stigwood Music, Inc.
    (Unichappell Music, Inc., Administrator)
    International copyright secured
    ALL RIGHTS RESERVED
    Used by permission.
    Selection used in Chapter 6. From *Saturday Night Fever:*

    Its all right, its okay
    You can look the other way.
    Life goin nowhere, somebody help me
    Life goin nowhere, somebody help me.
    I'm stayin alive
    I'm stayin alive
    Whether you're a brother, or whether you're a mother,
    You're stayin alive.

NTL Institute's Reading Book. Mimeographed, 1967. Used with permission from Learning Resources Corporation, San Diego.

Scott, W. G., and Mitchell, T. R. *Organizational theory: A structural and behavioral analysis*, rev. ed. Homewood, Ill.: Richard D. Irwin, Inc., 1972, p. 23.

Thayer, F. C. *An end to hierarchy! An end to competition!* New York: Franklin Watts, Inc., 1973, pp. 76–77.

Whisler, T. L. *Impact of computers on organizations.* New York: Holt, Rinehart & Winston, 1970.

To Kathy

CONTENTS

FOREWORD

Dr. William Kraus has written an exuberantly normative book
heralding the transformation of our organizational structures
(and hence the lives of those working in human institutions)
from competitive to cooperative value systems. He describes in
great detail, drawing on examples to further his thesis, the
vicissitudes, character, and values of competitive/hierarchical
bureaucracies and those that are cooperative/horizontal types.

It's clear that Kraus believes in collaborative systems and
that change is needed desperately, since he and many others
whom he quotes feel that competitive practices are doing a
great deal of damage. Human relations, morale; productivity,
innovative capacity all suffer and the competitive model is, in
general, eroding the quality of work life.

The exuberance and moral imperative expressed throughout the book as well as the historical examples cited provide a
fascinating perspective on the problems of large-scale organizations and the ways the organizations can be restructured to

bring about a better integration that now seems to exist between employees' basic human needs and organizational goals.

At the same time, Dr. Kraus could say more about how we get from the venerable competitive model to the hoped-for collaborative one. The phenomenon that there are significant personality and cultural predispositions for each value system is accounted for, but under certain conditions one system may be more productive than another.

The book will stir up controversy: it is sure to be enshrined by some and vilified by others. However, it certainly does create the proper focus and archetypes for further debate and, hopefully, more research.

Warren Bennis
Professor of Research
University of Southern California

ACKNOWLEDGMENTS

I never realized how important other people besides the author were in the creation of a book until I had finished work on this one. By the time I had finished the book, I found the list of those to whom I was indebted too long to include everyone here; yet I wish to acknowledge by name some of the individuals who have been important in this process.

My wife, Kathy, provided the support and encouragement needed to keep me at the typewriter week after week, believed in my ideas, and sees them as a positive contribution to a changing society. My twins, Jamie and Julie, let me work, but on the day I finished the first draft and put the card table away, went running through the house screaming for joy, "Daddy finished his book!"

A very special thanks to Fred Finch and Don Carew, who kept me going and got me started in the first place; to Bob White, another believer; and to Carol Schrieber for having faith in my writing and in the worth of my perspective.

I also thank, as I remember with fondness, all the members of the Applied Behavioral Science Alliance, especially Chuck Hamilton, Edie Seashore, Herb Shepard, Wally Sikes, and Orion Worden, who helped me to clarify my own thinking in the area of collaboration while they worked from a value system that exemplified that model.

My very special thanks to Janet Kean for her editing, to Judy Snyder for her research assistance, to Cece Trachey for her typing of the first draft, and to Pam Bartel for her typing of the final draft.

Thanks also to the people who contributed case material: Jean Charland, Kathy Kraus, Gary Lehrman, Jack Montgomery, Lee Scott, and Arlene Snyder.

Important also were people in the Hartford, Connecticut, business community who provided feedback on an issue that clearly affects them in their daily work lives and gave me encouragement to continue pursuing my ideas. Special thanks to Jack Montgomery, who as a friend and a colleague gave me a first reaction to my manuscript.

I can't stop without a clear statement of thanks to my parents, Alice Hobolth and Arnold Kraus, who supported me through the earlier struggles.

My sincere thanks to all of you and to many unlisted colleagues and friends who believe in the positive value of collaboration.

Chapter 1

WHY COLLABORATION AT ALL

If man is incapable of changing reality, he adjusts himself instead. Adaptation is behavior characteristic of the animal sphere; exhibited by man, it is symptomatic of his dehumanization (Freire, 1973, p. 4).

Today, the task of overcoming our lack of democratic experience through experiences in participation still awaits us (Freire, 1973, p. 59).

They are playing a game. They are playing at not playing a game. If I show them I see they are, I shall break the rules and they will punish me. I must play their game, of not seeing I see the game (Laing, 1970).

Most organizations and social systems in Western society currently utilize hierarchical structures resulting in competition as a major value system. This competitive value system is often perceived to be consistent with a behavioral pattern of competitive behaviors. This competitive pattern is then taken as evidence of the need for a hierarchical structure in order that human kind's animal instincts can be controlled and channeled into productive enterprises. Some gentle form of coercion in the form of hierarchically induced and reinforced authority is slipped into place with appropriate rationalizations implying that of course these are appropriate—it's only natural!

I am proposing an alternative value system, an alternative set of processes and structures, and a new set of behaviors that would be appropriate for these new dynamics. The term for these new dynamics, which I will use throughout the book, is collaboration. Collaboration has at its core, noncompetitive cooperative behavior and nonhierarchical structures and processes in organizations.

The collaborative model supports and reinforces individual development and contributions. It also provides a framework to organize a social system. The collaborative model assumes people are inherently good, want to be productive, and can utilize an organizational system to further their own ends as well as those of the organization.

It further presupposes the need for radical changes in current organizational structures and practices as a necessary, although insufficient, condition for a new framework to become operational.

It also requires differential value systems, encompassing resocialization on the part of individuals, and major change in expectations and assumptions toward their social systems on their part and on the part of social systems toward individuals immersed in them.

The collaborative model is a hard-nosed model in that it is not simple or easy to implement.

It particularly necessitates a great deal of energy and effort to understand the implications and to become involved in the transition from a competitive model to a collaborative one.

COLLABORATION: A PRELIMINARY DEFINITION

Before proceeding further, it is appropriate to focus on a preliminary definition of collaboration for two reasons:

First, to attempt to define collaboration in a concise fashion results in a superficial definition. Collaboration involves perception, values, expectations, assumptions, behaviors, structures, processes, and outcomes. Indeed, a variety of complex variables must be covered in a single definition.

A second meaningful reason revolves around the development and emergent nature of the concept of collaboration. Although the term itself is not new, there has been little systematic work on defining the term and its ramifications in regard to major changes in organizational functioning.

There is still much to conceive, much to learn, and much to design and implement before the term collaboration will have a concise, systematic definition or description.

This is not to apologize to the reader for a lack of specificity in the definition; rather it's an explanation of the complexities and subtleties that will be encountered in the remainder of this book.

I would also point out that this preliminary focus on a definition of collaboration is just that—a preliminary focus—and that I will discuss all the components from a variety of perspectives throughout subsequent chapters.

Collaboration is a cooperative venture based on shared power and authority. It is nonhierarchial in nature. It assumes power based on a knowledge or expertise as opposed to power based on role or role function. It utilizes Theory Y assumptions about people.

People who are able to function in a collaborative way are those individuals who are aware of themselves: who they are, what they stand for, what their skills are, and what "pushes their buttons."

They are aware of their own mechanisms for need satisfaction and thus do not exploit others in a destructive fashion. They do not need their role or title to tell them who they are or what they can do, or even what they should do. Their identity is not solely based on who or what they are in an organization.

They do, however, behave in ways that demonstrate caring and concern for others in a nonmanipulative fashion. They care because of what the other person gains, not because of their own personal gain. At the same time, they do not sacrifice themselves in the process, i.e., they are not great "rescuers."

Collaborative organizations are those that:

—are based on Theory Y assumptions;
—utilize shared power and responsibility;
—involve a high degree of participative decision-making;
—are nonhierarchical in nature;
—focus *less* on *roles* and *more* on *functions*;
—involve decisions by function rather than by role;
—foster decisions being made by those who must implement them;
—are operated as open systems;
—recognize the uniquely ordered perceptual field of each individual;
—have built-in mechanisms for self-renewal (both individual and organizational);
—recognize the need for continual ongoing processes of feedback, evaluation, and modification (both individual and organizational);
—recognize the importance of *process* as well as input and output;

—foster mechanisms for building, recognizing, and supporting interdependence;

—recognize and support multigroup membership;

—utilize conflict resolution strategies based on problem-solving methodologies rather than arbitrary resolution or political methodologies;

—foster a high degree of individual control over the immediate work environment;

—function with a common value base that influences organizational and individual behavior; and

—share a common frame of reference with regard to the appropriateness and utility of a collaborative mode of operating.

COLLABORATION: SEE TREASON

One of the real difficulties in writing in the area of collaboration is that to begin is to acknowledge the challenges to the basic nature, values, and structure of Western society. To challenge these is often to be seen as irrational or treasonous. It is also seen as naive and very idealistic. It is often seen as having some interesting ideas; some ideas that clearly are related to feelings people have about their organizational life, but that are simply not practical.

In the initial stages of research and data collection for this work it seemed most appropriate to start with the library. I was at the University of Massachusetts, Amherst, at the time and thus used that card catalog. (I have no reason to believe it would not be substantially the same at most large university libraries.) The initial word on which a reference search was begun was "collaboration." The catalog said: Collaboration: See Treason.

Imagine my surprise as I looked around and found additional references to Authority, Despotism, Fascism, National Socialism, Totalitarianism, and Authoritarianism; not one reference to cooperation or any entry into the behavioral sciences.

It is also interesting—if not depressing—that Hampton, Summer, and Webber in *Organizational Behavior and the Practice of Management* refer the reader to sections on collusion in that portion of the index referring to collaboration. I did find some brief bit of solace in the dictionary definition of collaboration, which is "to labor together."

This experience came to have a great deal of impact as I worked on projects collaboratively with others. I began to observe the depth of socialization and the strength of the reward systems around competitive and hierarchical systems. I began to develop clear perspectives on what Heinlein referred to in the title of his science fiction novel: *Stranger in a Strange Land*. These feelings became very clear to me in a project labeled the Applied Behavioral Science Alliance (Kraus et al., 1977) and again in a joint writing venture with several other authors.

This venture involved a special issue of a journal about collaboration in work settings. After much of the work had been done in a collaborative fashion — at least, with this value base and these structures and processes — two people moved to a hierarchical model with themselves "in charge." Ostensibly they did so because an outside board didn't understand what we were doing and because "it just had to be this way to get the job done." Such irony for an issue about collaboration and nonhierarchical functioning.!

COMPETITION AS COUNTERFEIT BEHAVIOR

It is my belief that competition is counterfeit behavior. In addition, hierarchical structure is that structure that fosters competitive behavior, and, hence, must also be labeled counterfeit.

This behavior (competitive and hierarchical) is coun- terfeit because it does not maximize productivity, does not maximize development of individual potential, and is gen- erally inconsistent with goals and purposes professed by the organization. Much research has indicated that competitive behavior is of limited usefulness in organizational settings, and that the carry-over into other settings makes it extremely difficult for people to cooperate when cooperation is indeed extremely appropriate behavior.

Hierarchy is the major structural component that creates and reinforces competitive behavior in organiza- tional settings. Pirsig (1974) addresses this issue when he discusses the notion of hierarchy. He indicates that since ancient times hierarchy has been a basic structure for all Western knowledge.

> Kingdoms, empires, churches, armies have all been struc- tured into hierarchies. Modern businesses are so structured. Tables of contents of reference material are so structured, mechanical assemblies, computer software, all scientific and technical knowledge is so structured—so much so that in some fields such as biology, the hierarchy of phylum-order- class-genus-species is almost an icon. (p. 93)

Even though Pirsig discusses the concept of hierarchy as a classification framework, the point still is made. The notion of a hierarchy is used in an organization as a classifier as well — it classifies human beings into greater and lesser niches. Hierarchy is indeed internalized so much in Western culture that it is difficult for most people to move outside of the framework to examine some of the ramifications of its conceptual adoption.

Hierarchy assumes one person is ultimately responsible for decisions and resource utilization. It also assumes that individuals below a given person on the hierarchical ladder

will strive for that job since major reward systems in organizations involve a movement upward in the hierarchical
structure. Competitive behavior is contrary to the development within the group or organization of feelings of responsibility for decisions, of creativity, and even of loyalty to the
organization (loyalty is one of those behavior patterns in
which organizations indicate an interest).

Hierarchical structure is based on the value assumption
of scarce resources. If the assumption of scarce resources is
indeed true, hierarchical structure and competitive behavior
are indeed appropriate. If resources are indeed scarce one
would be foolish not to make strong attempts to get and
maintain as much of a resource base as possible, since it is
clear that the amount of resource control is a powerful
influence in organizational life.

I would maintain, however, that the resources primarily used in the competitive struggle are those resources that
are not scarce at all, but are, in fact, unlimited.

The specific resources to which I refer are psychological
resources. These include such things as status, prestige, creativity, concern for others, roles, power, and understanding.
These resources are the ones over which people compete in
organizations, the ones that are distributed via the hierarchical structure in organizations.

Organizations are fundamentally composed of individuals, groups, and social systems, all of which are lodged in
an environment, and all of these variables interact in an
interdependent fashion. Organizations also possess a
number of processes.

Two of the most important of these processes are
decision-making/problem-solving and communication/in-
formation flow. Both are influenced greatly by the variables
mentioned previously.

It is precisely because of this definition of organizations
that a collaborative order is appropriate. Collaboration involves *not* the lack or absence of power; rather, it connotes

power shared between individuals. Collaboration involves shared or collective decision-making power. This facilitates a *functional* focus rather than a power or authority focus.

COMPETITION AS AN IDEAL

Competition in Western society has become so ingrained in the fabric of our culture that it has become a primary value.

> The competitive ideal as it is now practiced is out of hand and promises to be among the nation's most resistant menaces. If it continues under its present guises, the ruination of the nation is inevitable and will proceed along with a growing neuroticism of its people and the threat of world destruction (Nichols, 1975 p. 92).

Nichols (1975) further states that competition derives partly from the intellectual tendency to make comparisons. The result is that the self is often compared with others rather than focusing on its own uniqueness regardless of what others do.

The competitive ideal, the competitive spirit, is often taught as an end in itself.

> Those who approach it with unlimited praise, inculcating it in little boys and girls and preaching it to the young people on the brink of their careers, fail to see that competing has an amoral coloration and that without this recognition it will be pursued with no thought of the harm it does as long as men (and women) think it an ultimate value in its own right (Nichols, 1975, p. 91).

Ashley Montagu (1962) also challenges the commonly held view that competition is the "lifeblood of a nation." He suggests that America has achieved its greatness *in spite* of competition rather than because of it.

Competition in the business setting is considered necessary for a healthy economy. Competition has existed, but it has not been healthy for small business owners. Rather, it has facilitated the wide spread monopolistic enterprises and attitudes in America.

Kefauver (1965) stated: "In our society the practices of monopoly are often secreted behind a front of 'competition'." He pointed specifically to the oil and automobile industries as outrageous examples (particularly interesting in these times of spiraling gas prices) and included a powerful historical perspective on the Ford Motor Company.

Many figures of national prominence have embraced competition as a national ethic. These include John Connally (1972) and Richard Nixon (1971) as well as figures in the sports world. The Olympics can be viewed as the ultimate in destructive competition (Chavoor and Davidson, 1973), as can most major sports (Boslooper and Hayes, 1973).

Nichols (1975) in his book, *Men's Liberation*, strongly points out that:

> The liberation of men demands a restoration of balance in such fields as have been ravaged by the competitive ideal. Until this balance is found, men, and particularly American men, will suffer individually and collectively. It is high time that parents and educators gave more careful consideration to the matter before sending men into the world, impelled hopelessly toward nothing more than competition and winning (p. 108).

Certainly as more and more women enter organizations at all levels, the same words apply to them as well.

Some individuals are talking about the need for major revisions in our social structures. Szent-Gyorgyi (1970), a Nobel Laureate, writes:

> We live in a new cosmic world which man was not made for. His survival now depends on how well and how fast he can

adapt himself to it, rebuilding all his ideas, all his social and
economic and political structures (p. 17).

Competition and hierarchy were initially useful and,
in fact, quite functional. In the early days of the industrial
revolution, where skills were not widely distributed and
knowledge was not shared by a diverse and heterogeneous
population, the hierarchy was functional.

However, these institutions don't die and therein lies
the difficulty. Szent-Gyorgyi (1970) very elegantly describes
the process when he says: "These institutions begin to serve
their own interests rather than social needs. As time goes by
the social needs and philosophy change, but the institutions
don't.

> In our society, for example, most positions of eminence are
> filled competitively, and hence, require a permanently in-
> tense and narrow motivation. Success is achieved by becom-
> ing a machine — an engine without a governor, single-
> mindedly directed to winning competitions and aggrandiz-
> ing the ego (p. 122).

Many writers, including Slater (1974) and Thompson
(1967), talk about competition in the international political
sphere, in the sense of competing for shares in a limited
market. While the dynamics of competition are in operation
in the economic sphere, more effort in this writing will focus
on competition between individuals and groups for such
rewards as power, prestige, status, position, and on competition as it is fostered and imbedded in organizational structures and processes.

ORGANIZATIONS AS SOCIAL INVENTIONS

Many writers in the literature on organizations focus on
the notion that organizations are merely inventions in the

minds of individuals. They are seen as perceptual phenomena created as survival mechanisms in a world that might
appear incomprehensible without them (Bavelas, 1960; Silverman, 1970; Greenfield, 1973).

Bavelas pointedly states that "human organizations are
not biological organisms; they are social inventions" (1960,
p. 498). Greenfield further states:

> the kinds of organizations we live in derive not from their
> structure but from attitudes and experiences we bring to
> organizations from the wider society in which we live. Organ-
> izational change, then, requires more than structural change;
> it requires changes in the meanings and purposes that indi-
> viduals learn within their society (1973), pp. 558-559).

I can only partially agree with Greenfield. It is clear that
our life experiences influence our perceptual frameworks; in
turn, our behaviors are consistent with these frameworks.

However, I would maintain that these behaviors result
from our experiences with systematic socialization processes
regarding the likely rewarded behaviors in organizational
contexts. We are lead to behave in a competitive fashion by
our exposure and growth in hierarchical structures and processes; these structures and processes exist in many real
ways—even if merely because we all agree (perceive) that
they exist.

The Perceptionists would have us believe that organizations are merely figments of our perceptual imagination.
The Organizationalists, on the other hand, would have us
believe that organizations exist as purely rational entities
with clearly defined goals and structures and clearly operating processes for attaining these goals. The Perceptionists
see perceptual processes and life experiences as independent
variables. The Organizationalists see structure and organizational processes as independent variables.

The collaborative model is a transcendent conceptual
framework, which recognizes the validity of both the Percep-

tionists and the Organizationalists. It's merely a matter of where the distinction is made. In trying to understand life in organizations, the often repeated query "Which comes first, the chicken or the egg?" is encountered. In order to understand the process, you have to become aware that both the chicken and the egg are inherently intertwined in the same process.

To change organizational life as it is known today, we must focus on and ultimately change perception as well as structure, socialization, values, rewards, and stimuli.

The next chapter will examine some of the historical roots of the competitive model, as well as the movement of conflict as an independent concept to a concept intrinsically intertwined with competition.

Chapter 2

HISTORICAL DEVELOPMENT OF COMPETITION AND THE EMERGENCE OF CONFLICT

As I discussed in the previous chapter, assumptions held about organizations and social systems, and the value systems individuals hold about other individuals and organizations, influence the concepts, design, and implementation of organizations in Western society.

This chapter examines the development of competition from an historical perspective and focuses on the movement toward the integration of conflict into the competitive sphere of influence. It describes the transition of conflict from a political base to a physiological one.

The resulting concept of conflict frequently includes competition as its core. Thus, formal organizations supposedly designed to limit conflict actually limit competition.

At the same time, those formal organizations (really, informal ones as well) that are built upon a hierarchical model, produce competitive behavior patterns and accompanying beliefs in the positive value of competition. Hierarchical organizations are therefore perpetuating the very value system and behavior pattern they are theoretically in existence to control.

These phenomena will be discussed in more detail in subsequent chapters. For now the important point to keep in mind is that beneath dynamics of conflict in organizational settings lurks the ever present specter of competition.

Conflict in organizational settings has at its core competition for some resource that is *perceived* to be scarce. Status, prestige, power, and influence are among those resources commonly perceived as scarce. This perceived scarcity also emerges because of a behavior pattern and a set of philosophical and conceptual assumptions about the nature of conflict.

Conflict is believed to be influenced by its major component, competition. This competitive value system has emerged from hundreds of years of thinking, has become strongly wedded to our beliefs about the nature and inevitability of conflict as both a given in organizational settings and as the essence of the human condition itself.

COMPETITION: ROOTS IN CONFLICT THEORY AND POLITICAL SCIENCE

Early versions of societal foundations rested with Polybius (Greek historian, c.205–125 B.C.) with his focus on conflict. He wrote that conflict among people must ultimately be resolved by the development of a government based on a combination of kingship, aristocracy, and democracy. The Romans, particularly Lucretius and Horace, applied Polybius's philosophy, maintaining that all things originated in conflict. Livy also sang the praises of conflict as a value in Roman expansion to centralize power and bring a blessed peace (Martindale, 1960).

Conflict theory emerged again with Ibn Khaldun

(1332–1406), who fostered the beginning of sociological theory as well. Khaldun argued that social phenomenon resulted from laws similar to those found in natural phenomenon. Khaldun felt individuals always banded together for survival but that trouble developed as

> there arises the need of a restraining force to keep men off each other in view of their animal propensities for aggression and oppression of others.
>
> The restraint must therefore be constituted by one man, who wields power and authority with a firm hand and thus prevents anyone from attacking anyone else, i.e., by a sovereign. Sovereignty is therefore peculiar to man, suited to his nature and indispensable to his existence. (Khaldun, 1950, p. 101)

As with Polybius, Khaldun believed that power was concentrated in the hands of a few with estrangement between ruler and subject resulting from concentration.

The next theorist who had major impact on Western thinking was the Italian statesman Niccolo Machiavelli (1469–1527), whose best known work, *The Prince*, and his most profound work, *Discourses on the First Ten Books of Livy* both contained the same theoretical framework of human nature. Human nature was basically evil and men were only good when they were constrained. Man's evil didn't always show itself, but it was always present even if hidden. Machiavelli observed that

> Men are bad and ever ready to display their vicious nature whenever they may find occasion for it.
>
> Poverty and hunger make men industrious, and law makes men good. (Machiavelli, 1948, p. 117)

Again, we see the beginnings of the building of nations, states, and systems based on values that have carried into today's thinking.

Jean Bordin (1530-1596) was another person who contributed much to our present view of the world. Bordin, a Frenchman, believed human behaviors were governed by basic laws of nature. He believed that every association of people involves subjection of some members to others. The Englishman Thomas Hobbes (1588-1679) continued in the same spirit as earlier writers. Hobbes indicated that the "natural relations of an individual to every other are competition, distrust, and the struggle for prestige" (Martindale, 1960, p. 138).

David Hume (1711-1776) was in agreement with previous conflict theorists and much of today's hierarchical focus in organizations might well be traced to some of Hume's notions. He says for example that there is an

> easiness with which the many are governed by the few: and the implicit submission with which men resign their own sentiments, and passions to those of their rulers. (Hume, 1907, pp. 109-110)

Hume focused on the interaction between consent and force, but usually indicated that social systems emerged and were maintained by some sort of force.

Two additional theorists, Adam Ferguson (1723-1816) and Robert Turgot (1727-1781) of Scottish and French descent respectively, continued in the same empirical track and with the same notions as Hume.

Gradually an attitude emerged that posited conflict as inevitable, resulting from the basic nature of human beings as bad, greedy, and needing to be controlled by others. Competition was seen as innate within the individual rather than resulting from social structure and processes, or as a behavior pattern that was an outcome of an individual's interaction with social systems and processes of organizing.

COMPETITION: ROOTS IN CONFLICT THEORY AND ECONOMICS

In the eighteenth century, conflict theorists moved into the arena of economic phenomena. The physiocrats focused on the agricultural class as the important one. The state was to assist the natural order of things (as seen by the agriculturalists).

In *The Wealth of Nations*, Adam Smith expanded and modified these early views by placing the source of all value on labor. Smith's major additions were that (1) competition should be completely free in economic affairs, for only then could maximum productivity be attained; and (2) natural forces will deal with requirements of both groups and individuals so that the government sphere should be reduced (Martindale, 1960).

Adam Smith and the physiocrats laid the foundation of classical economics. They continued the focus on the *positive nature of conflict* (political conflict was seen as positive by Turgot and Ferguson); in fact, they expanded it to be widely applicable. "Economic competition is the great agency of efficiency in the production of the necessities of life" (Martindale, 1960, p. 144).

Thomas Malthus (1766–1834) is recognized for raising competition to its current revered position. Malthus indicated a tendency for life to reach beyond the available nourishment or population to increase beyond available resources. He postulated the geometric increase in population rate, and thus reinforced the theory that *all competition ultimately becomes competition to survive.*

Martindale succinctly summarizes the thinking at this point:

> The detail concern here is with the sharp, hard turn given to the meaning of competition as a form of conflict central to economic behavior, and with the consequences of this conflict for the conduct of society, the standard of living, the condition of labor, and the social classes. (1960, p. 146)

COMPETITION: ROOTS IN CONFLICT THEORY AND BIOLOGY

Charles Darwin was greatly influenced by Malthus:

> In October, 1838, that is, fifteen months after I had begun my systematic inquiry, I happened to read for amusement, *Malthus on Population*. Being well prepared to appreciate the struggle for existence which everywhere goes on, from long continued observation of the habits of animals and plants, it at once struck me that under these circumstances favorable variations would tend to be preserved, and unfavorable ones to be destroyed. The result would be the formation of new species. Here, then, I had at last got a theory by which to work. (Darwin, 1887)

Darwin had elevated the theory of competition for limited resources to a biological level. The idea of struggle for existence and the survival of the fittest provided the needed conceptual framework. *A mechanism that placed the ultimate importance on efficiency* was born.

Conflict has changed from a variable outside the mainstream of thinking and conceptualization to a variable that is taken as a given in much modern thinking, cultural and societal values, and resultant organizational structures and processes.

In fact, conflict has been transformed into competition. Competition has become the major process through which conflict is maintained and flourishes.

COMPETITION AND SOCIAL DARWINISM

Competition found a home in several types of social Darwinism. Social Darwinism is based on Darwin's notion of the survival of the fittest, with the responsibility to "help the process" along, resting with certain individuals or segments of society.

> Marxism was a conflict ideology projected in the names and interests of the proletariat. Social Darwinism was a conflict ideology projected in the name of the upper strata of bourgeois society. Marxism's external program was the worldwide union of the proletariat; social Darwinism's external program was imperialism ("manifest destiny," the "white man's burden"). (Martindale, 1960, p. 174)

Competition has grown from a small component of a larger concept of conflict theory to an integral part of conflict theory. In fact, competition is more than a natural outgrowth of conflict — it is the very essence of conflict. The perspective that conflict always has competition at its core gains further momentum when one examines behavior in the context of organizational settings.

As will be seen in more depth in subsequent chapters, hierarchy is a major perpetuator and reinforcer of competitive behavior. This process of perpetuation by organizational structures, which are hierarchical in nature, leads further to the conclusion that conflict, with its core component of competition, is inevitable in this society. This is not perhaps an inevitability in any fixed, unchangeable, or core fashion, but rather a series of interactions between historical development, perceptual internalization, and reinforcement by expectation and formal organizational structure.

COMPETITION: ROOTS IN SOCIOLOGICAL THEORY

Many social scientists continue to analyze and present competition as if it were outside the mainstream of organizational life.

Park and Burgess (1924) give a glimpse of this thinking in their presentation of the relationships between social structures and the social processes of competition, conflict, accommodation, and assimilation:

Social Process	Social Order
Competition	The economic equilibrium
Conflict	The political order

Accommodation   Social organization
Assimilation   Personality and the cultural
                            heritage

                            (Park and Burgess, 1924,
                            p. 520)

It is important to note than competition is seen as a part of the economic equilibrium, but is not seen as a critical social process in social organizations.

Again, a failure to recognize competition as a vital part of social systems is evident. It is vital as both an independent variable, influencing the nature of organizations and expectations about organizations, and also as a process variable and a dependent variable.

This makes for an interesting situation in which one variable is both an independent variable and a dependent variable. Another way of stating this is to view competition as both a stimulus and a response, with hierarchy serving as a reinforcer of the response. This may be stretching a strict utilization of behaviorist terminology, but in this case, it is applicable as a descriptive tool for analysis of the complexities of behavior in organizational settings.

There are a variety of other sociologists who view competition and hierarchy as inevitable in an organizational society. These include Davis & Moore (1945), Tumin (1953, 1963), Fallding (1963), and Moore (1963), all of whom state either explicitly or imply implicitly that hierarchy (stratification is their term) is inevitable. There is also an implicit notion in much of the writing in sociology that competition is also inevitable; although the link to hierarchy is often not clearly specified.

DEMOCRACY, POLITICS, AND THE GROWTH OF HIERARCHY

Aristotle (translated, 1962) is often thought of as a major proponent of democracy. He may well be, but his *a priori* commitment was to hierarchy and he saw society as equivalent to a military structure with hierarchy as its core organizing principle. Early philosophers clearly made the distinction between those who ruled and those who were ruled. Rousseau and Hobbes also focused on hierarchy.

> Rousseau's distinction between rulers and ruled was precisely the same as that of Aristotle and Hobbes. Ironically, Hobbes saw hierarchical structures as necessary to prevent individuals from behaving as persons, while Rousseau saw them as necessary to enable individuals to become persons. (Thayer, 1973, p. 62)

To this day democracy is viewed as having some roots in competition. Schumpeter (1950) clearly expresses this view as he discusses competition as a component in the democratic prócess.

> The democratic method is that institutional arrangement for arriving at political decisions in which individuals acquire the power to decide by means of a competitive struggle for the people's vote (p. 269)

Thayer (1973) has summarized the predominant political models of democratic government (Figure 2-1). Note that each clearly perpetuates the concept of a *hierarchy* with distance between the superiors and the subordinates. There is no notion of interdependence or much real shared power, leadership, or control. It is little wonder, then, that the organizations that grow out of the entity of a political state and a set of cultural and social values indeed contain and perpetuate many of the same notions.

Perhaps Thayer (1973) states with greatest impact the prevalence of the change:

> Our system of representative government is designed only to preserve hierarchy, and our economic system is based on the ideal of competition. Yet neither hierarchy nor competition

Rulers

```
R   C
O   O
T   M
A   M
T   A
E   N
    D
```

Ruled

Aristotle

Citizens

```
C
O
M
M
A
N
D
```

Representatives

Rousseau (misinterpretation)
Lowi (sometimes)
Tullock "Public Choice"

Elites

```
A   C
C   O
C   M
E   M
S   A
S   N
    D
```

Citizens

Dahl "Pluralism"
Truman "Groups"

Representatives

```
E   C
L   O
E   M
C   M
T   A
    N
    D
```

Citizens

"Accountability"
Pateman, Rousseau

Sovereign

```
B   C
E   O
C   M
O   M
M   A
E   N
    D
```

(some) Citizens

Hobbes
Madison
Lowi (sometimes)
Riskanen "Public Choice"

Elites

```
C
O
M
M
A
N
D
```

Citizens

Mills, Hunter "Power Elite"

Figure 2-1: Adapted from Thayer's (1973) *Models of "Democratic" Government*, pp. 76-77.

has a place in our future. For both compel us to repress ourselves and each other. The organizational revolution is an attempt to end repression, and the alienation that accompanies it (p. 3)

INTERACTION BETWEEN THE INDIVIDUAL AND THE ORGANIZATION

An outgrowth of the view of competition residing in the individual is a widely held concept that human behavior can be explained and predicted almost wholly by using the individual as the unit of analysis with almost total disregard for the social context within which that behavior occurs.

A more recent focus on the organization as the unit of analysis has led to an examination of the context within which behavior occurs in an attempt to analyze the interaction between the individual and that context (organization).

Even those theorists who focused on the formal organization as the unit of analysis still assumed that competition was an individual attribute brought into the situation from outside of it, rather than one that was immersed in the context (organization) itself.

RATIONAL BUREAUCRACY

Regarding the organization as the unit of analysis, the writings of Max Weber (1946) are relevant. Weber proposed a rational systems view with clear lines of authority, clear differentiated functions, and clear responsibilities established at each vertical and horizontal level within the organization (hierarchy). This served the purpose of clarifying exact spheres of influence for each person within the system, and provided for clear procedures to establish accountability to accompany responsibility.

Weber also included a "waterfall" notion of authority,

which flowed from the top down at the discretion of those at the top. This was based on a fundamental premise of a limited amount of power and authority so that those who had it discretely shared it in ways that allowed them to retain fundamental control. Those who shared the power could easily take it away again if tasks were not completed according to the prescribed organizational pattern.

The rational bureaucracy of Weber did serve the function of clarifying responsibilities and establishing limits on favoritism and blatant coercion as mainstays of organizational life. It attempted to place emphasis on performance to control blatant competition, since competition was seen as a "given" that each individual brought to a situation. Since winning or losing would not be relevant variables, it was thought that by making every aspect of organizational functioning crystal clear, there would be no place for competition. The only appropriate behavior pattern would be that specified in the situation.

THE HUMAN RELATIONS MOVEMENT

All thinking about the world of work in organizations has not been unidirectional. The human relations movement, as reflected by the Hawthorne studies, was an attempt to respond to some dynamics of work in organizations other than the classical management functions of planning, directing, controlling, and organizing.

Ironically, these early attempts (some of which persist even now) fall short of an examination of the impact of the central organizing theme of hierarchy. The human relations movement attempted to remove power and control from previous perceptions about work in organizations by hoping it would go away, or by pretending it didn't exist. This framework failed to deal with competition and hierarchy; by failing to respond to them, it merely conspired in their perpetuation. More recently, efforts to examine the effects of competition and hierarchy in organizations have appeared in literature about the world of work in organizations (Thayer, 1973; Steele, 1975; Ingalls, 1976).

THE ENDURING NATURE OF HIERARCHY

The endurance of hierarchy in today's organizations rests on deep and long-standing foundations. It has developed and flourished with much philosophical support and little questioning of a thorough nature. It has roots in philosophy, psychology, and political science; like its counterpart, democracy, it is taken for granted in Western society.

The interaction of hierarchy and competition will be developed more fully in subsequent chapters. Organizations, as structures that generate, facilitate, and reinforce competition, and the impact of these structured processes on individual behavior, will be examined.

Again, it is important to note that hierarchy is the major structural variable that reinforces competition as a value system and facilitates its implementation as a behavioral pattern.

CONFLICT AND COMPETITION

This chapter began with the premise that competition has become entangled with conflict, resulting in conflict always having competition as its essential ingredient. Conflict as it exists within the framework of formal organizations and social systems almost always is synonymous with competition. This situation exists because of socialization processes to which individuals have been exposed and have supported.

These socialization processes include:

1. Tying competition to the individual and
2. Teaching competition as a positive value system and behavior pattern.

Competition is further a part of conflict because:

1. Organizations perpetuate and foster competition through hierarchy, even though they are designed to limit it, and
2. Conflict is resolved in win-lose ways by utilizing the hierarchy of authority in the organization

Conflict in and of itself is not bad. This is often espoused in the literature of the behavioral sciences as well as from individuals commenting on the human condition. It is often stated that conflict is a learning process that ensues when emerging from a painful experience or process. This only occurs after the conflict has been worked through or understood in terms of its initiating and perpetuating dynamics.

If, as has been previously postulated, conflict is intertwined with competition and resolved in a win-lose fashion (by definition), then confronting conflict results more in learning about competition than in developing appreciation of individual differences or learning about one's self.

Much of the literature from the behavioral sciences specifies that there are three fundamental methodologies that can be used in resolving conflict: (1) win-lose strategies, (2) negotiation strategies, and (3) problem-solving strategies.

One is "supposed" to use conflict constructively by analyzing the causes of the conflict and "selecting" the appropriate conflict resolution strategy. This all sounds good, but the reality in today's organizations is that competition is such a major process with which to be reckoned that the only "sensible" strategy is one that involves a win-lose mentality, or perhaps a negotiated settlement.

Conflict cannot be viewed as constructive in this milieu, but rather as a force that is ever present. One merely copes with conflict rather than resolves it in any long-lasting fashion. This coping emerges as the only viable option open to an individual who wishes to remain a mobile member of the organization.

Thus when you hear the phrase "Conflict can be a learning experience," remember that what the speaker or writer is really saying is that the learning comes from knowing and learning about how to play the organizational games with "class" or how to survive elegantly in an organizational setting.

One learns more about the process and sets of expectations that the organization has for its employees than one learns about the causes of the conflict itself. One also learns, even if not at a fully conscious level, that the causes of the conflict are an inherent part of the organizational framework; to challenge them is to "take on" the very system upon which one depends for his/her identity and survival.

> They are playing a game. They are playing at not playing a game. If I show them I see they are, I shall break the rules and they will punish me. I must play their game, of not seeing I see the game. (Laing, 1970)

Chapter 3

ORGANIZING FOR COMPETITION

Beware of people who believe. They aren't reliable players. All the same, one grows to like a good player on the other side of the board — it increases the fun. (Greene, 1978, p. 182)

This chapter examines the impact of organizing for competition on individual behavior patterns. As previously stated, the primary organizational mechanism perpetuating and reinforcing this competitive pattern is that of hierarchy. Power and control also interact with the competitive processes. Competition has become the mainstay of organizational functioning; in fact, it has become the technology of organizations.

Max Weber (1947) has pointed out that organizational actions are not a means toward some ultimate end, but rather are ends in themselves. A rather poignant example of this comes from a description of an upcoming budget process in one division of a large state university.

In order to obtain the best possible use of limited resources, the budget process will focus on the redistribution of resources within student affairs, especially in view of an inordinate

> number of new programs and no increase in allocations. Student affairs departments will essentially be competing against each other, which means where there are "winners," there will be comparable "losers." The budget process at all levels, therefore, requires a Solomon-like decision-making process based on the needs of the time and the strength or weakness of the program budget proposals. A popularity contest it is not. (Notes, 1973, p. 2)

Indeed, the outcome of this type of process ought to be quite predictable. Cohesion will develop during the competitive struggle, as will perceptions of the other group as the enemy.

The losers will blame someone or something outside of themselves for the outcome as they lose any cohesion that may have developed during the competitive struggle. Indeed, this is not exactly the outcome that organizations, most particularly universities, say they want in terms of their budget processes. It is also not consistent with other philosophical statements made about the ongoing nature of the organization.

Simon (1957) has described the interaction of competition and hierarchy by focusing on how each hierarchical level establishes the premises upon which the level below it will base its decisions.

One of the major premises that the next lower level grasps immediately is that it is better to be a winner than a loser. The budget process thus becomes one that is *really* about winning and losing rather than about a workable budget.

Each individual and each unit in the process feels that they were successful if they won and unsuccessful if they lost. A good budget package becomes a side product of a competitive process. George Orwell's (1946) words come to mind here as an outcome of the competitive process: "All animals are equal but some animals are more equal than others" (p. 123).

CASE NO. 1: COMPETITION:
THE CORPORATE CULLING CLUB

It would seem that anyone reading the many texts on organizational behavior would eventually understand that large corporate structure emulates itself after the military. Substituting a president or chairman of the board for commanding officer, conference officers for generals, and middle management for majors and lieutenants would be like interchanging Audi and Volkswagen Dasher parts. They are essentially the same. And, where such organizations are formed, one will almost always find the pyramid of control, with the commanding officer and generals at the top and the masses of privates, corporals, and sergeants at the bottom. There is nothing very earth shattering concerning these statements.

At the home office of The Dynamic Life Insurance Company (Dynamic), life goes on in the manner described above. The writer of this essay has been a member of this organization for ten years. He is essentially a staff aid to one of the majors in one of the divisions. (See how nicely the parts can be interchanged!) As a student of organizational behavior and a member of the corporate organization who is privy to confidential personnel information, a certain phenomenon has come to his attention that he believes is not readily understood by many people. The offshoot of the military pyramid, which was by *no* means premeditated in the minds of those who control, is competition. The end product of the phenomenon is a pervasive feeling among the masses at the bottom, and even the majority of middle management, that they cannot compete for the top prizes because competition is too fierce. They just give up. The people in control stay in control without having to stave off any attack by the enemy.

What good purpose, if any, does this intensity of competition have for the corporate organization?

As the intensity of competition goes up, the willingness of individuals to enter competition diminishes. In other words, competition is inversely proportional to the numbers of people willing to compete. And so, the corporation, without planning, has in its organizational structure a built-in culling club that only allows the strongest, the most cunning and sly, to reach top offices. Think of competition as analogous to the preditors of the Serengeti plain: The preditors keep the numbers down and the ecology in balance. Competition keeps the numbers down and balances the organizational structure so that the pryamid remains intact.

At Dynamic, competition is encouraged. It is looked upon as something healthy. In this light, one could probably surmise that the few in control view the phenomenon as having a good purpose for the organization. (It has a good purpose for them, the individuals in control.) For those aspiring to reach the next rung on the upward promotional ladder, it can be totally frustrating. The culling club effect increases at the higher level positions, and eventually, this leads most individuals to an unwillingness-to-compete attitude.

The real problem arises when we do an in-depth analytical study of what competition really means at the higher level positions within a corporation. In other words, is the corporation using the term competition when other variables enter into decision-making for filling vacant high level positions? Are employees made to believe that competition is really tough, when competition between skills, knowledge, and abilities of employees plays limited roles in the selection process?

The writer is sincerely afraid that a prevailing informal system exists within this company, and most other large corporate structures, that has a priority influence over the selection process. Employees seem to be informally judged. People in power make decisions concerning candidates for placement with little or no concrete objective information concerning the candidate's abilities. In no way is this competition in the spirit of its athletic definition. What we really see is decision-making by employees in control concerning other employees' advancement or progress within the company under the guise of clean and sportsmanlike competition. That's the game of corporate life. If one learns how to take advantage of it, it can be a helpful tool for growth and advancement. The majority of people in large private sector corporations are totally duped.

In conclusion, this writer believes that there is a culling force that exists within large corporate organizations designed around the military framework. This force, whether called competition or not, acts to solidify the pyramidal structure of control. As this force intensifies, individuals are less willing to enter the combat zone. More seems to be at stake when one loses, and the possibility of loss increases proportionately to the intensity of the culling effect.

The best possible advice would be for individual employees to identify the controlling force for what it really is in the organization. At that point, one can bring the force into objective focus, dealing with it, one hopes, on a more advantageous battleground.

The following section discusses research data regarding competition in organizational settings. It also integrates some of the comparative research done on competition and cooperation.

In fact, a great deal of research has not been conducted on competition as an independent variable. A short review of the prevailing research with an eye toward examining that research as it impacts collaboration in organizations should be helpful.

COMPETITION: RESEARCH DATA

There is little doubt that a group can be drawn closer together when competing with another group. However, there is little evidence that the seeking of mutually exclusive rewards even in the attainment of more general group goals is effective in producing an efficient environment for work (Deutsch, 1949a).

Morton Deutsch (1949a) did some of the earliest research on the effects of cooperation and competition. He reported that there was a higher degree of coordination, more friendliness, and more productivity in cooperative groups than in competitive ones. Hammond and Goldman (1961) found that both group and individual competition is less favorable for the group process than noncompetition. Jones and Vroom (1964) report that the greater the division of labor, the more effective the performance likely to result from cooperative conditions.

Mintz (1951) conducted a basic experiment demonstrating that of two similar groups, the group with a cooperative behavior pattern was more effective in completing the experimental task.

Hammond and Goldman (1961) have also indicated that noncompetition is more favorable to the group process.

Similar results were found by Myers (1962) when he examined the effects of two types of standards on intragroup relationships. ROTC students were organized into sixty three-person rifle teams. Half of the teams competed against low, medium, and high standards, while the other half competed against one another. The competition with other groups had the result of drawing teammates together, because a sense of unity was created by comparison (competition) with an external group.

Klein (1956) reported that members in groups with competitive goals would seek to "one up" each other, display hostile feelings, criticize, and withhold information.

On the other hand:

> Cooperative groups, in a task requiring collaborative activity, were found to have greater coordination of effort, greater attentiveness to members, orientations to the goal, orderliness of procedure, a sense of obligations to other members, and a better quality product (Chapin, 1957; Deutsch, 1960). (Quoted from Napier and Gershenfeld, 1973, pp. 117-118)

Deutsch (1959) has indicated that a cooperative relationship is more attractive to people in terms of group membership than a competitive one.

Napier and Gershenfield (1973) further emphasized that if a group will be rated on the basis of a team effort and if it has worked together to develop a team product, the members will be more friendly than in a competitive situation. When individual performance rating is used "there is less interpersonal relationship, more withholding of information or not volunteering of information, (and) fewer influence attempts" (p. 60).

Blau (1963) found that leadership that required collaboration rather than competition in an employment agency led to a more efficient and effective operation.

Lorsch and Lawrence (1965) reported the results of a pilot study focusing on ". . . obtaining collaboration and coordination between research, sales, and production specialists in two organizations producing basic plastic products" (p. 382). They emphasized two methods of improving collaboration. One is to establish a separate organizational unit, which has coordinating as its primary task, and the second ". . . is to use teams of committees in which the members have learned to *fight constructively* with each other." (p. 382; italics my own).

Both of these approaches for dealing with competition and improving collaboration result in much support for the continuation of the *status quo* in terms of organizational structure and functioning. Units that begin with a coordinating function soon perceive coordinating as a "higher order" function from the other functions in the various units. They have more information and soon use that additional information as a source of authority and power.

The use of committees that have learned to "fight constructively" may have some merit, except for one slight problem: that fighting will probably be done with a win-lose modality as a basic format, thus making competition, once again, a core component within conflict situations.

Once conflict emerges between groups, we tend to develop stereotypes that perpetuate the conflict. Blake and Mouton (1961) observed from their laboratory research on intergroup conflict

> two findings stemming from trends toward uniformities in membership behavior associated with protection of group interests which have unusual significance in determining barriers to the resolution of conflict between groups. They suggest that under competitive conditions members of one group perceive that they understand the others proposal when in fact they do *not*. Inadequate understanding makes it all the more difficult for competing groups to view each other's proposals realistically. Areas they share in common are likely to go unrecognized and in fact be seen as characteristic of one's own group only. Under conditions of competition, areas of true agreement will go undiscovered. (p. 252)

Research with Mexican and American children by Nelson and Kagan (1972) demonstrated that 10-year-old children in Los Angeles could not succeed in situations that required cooperation. Ten-year-old Mexican children, on the other hand, avoided the emphasis on competition and attained rewards by cooperating. This is some of the evidence that the competitive spirit is not a global phenomenon, however it is fostered in American schools (Johnson, Johnson & Bryant, 1973; Johnson, 1973; and Madsen and Conner, 1973).

Blake and Morton (1961) have also pointed out the ramifications of intergroup competition as it develops internally in many systems. When a system uses hidden information, stereotyping, preemptive maneuvering, and misleading actions, distrust is generated between that system and competitors, as well as between internal sub-units.

TRUST AND PROBLEM SOLVING

Napier and Gershenfeld (1973) reviewed much literature and pointed out that a competitive and hostile climate is likely to result whenever people who are engaged in problem-solving feel that the other side wants to reduce their power .

There is some experimentation in the area of competitive group games that demonstrates the tendencies to operate from a win-lose approach, attempting to maximize gains and minimize losses even if interdependence and cooperation are real options. There is usually a high degree of mistrust of motives of the other party (Deutsch, 1949b; Crombag, 1966; Hammond and Goldman, 1961). Even when both parties' gains can be maximized by cooperation, there is a clear tendency to develop a more independent and defensive strategy (Van Neumann and Morgenstern, 1947; Luce and Raiffa, 1957; and Edwards, 1967).

The result of this tendency to view situations competitively can turn a situation from one of interdependence to one in which secrecy, mistrust, and control prevail. The result is that vulnerability is unacceptable, the presentation of a strong face is important, and equity and compromise are sacrificed in favor of raw power (Scodel, et al., 1959; McClintock and McNeil, 1966).

COMPETITION AND COOPERATION

It seems appropriate here to examine the research that compares competition and cooperation, and to discuss some of the implications of these findings for organizational settings.

Miller and Hamblin (1963) reviewed 24 studies that compared competitive with cooperative groups. They found that 10 projects supported the proposition that cooperative groups were more productive while 14 studies found competitive groups to be more productive.

Miller and Hamblin suggest that competition and cooperation are not two ends of a continuum, but rather they should be broken into dimensions of *interdependence* (the degree to which group members need each other to complete the task) and *differential reward* (the degree to which compensation was given for individual effort).

Miller and Hamblin utilize a two-by-two table to present their dimensions.

| | | Interdependence | |
		High	Low
Differential Reward	High	1	3
	Low	2	4

They postulated that productivity would be higher in situations 2 and 3 than in 1 and 4 because there is a consistent relationship between effort and reward.

This theoretical conceptualization was tested by Miller and Hamblin and was generally supported. Also, in a reanalysis of the 24 studies in the topic they found that the results of 23 of them could be predicted from their formulation.

Although no such summary has been done for the effects of cooperation and competition on satisfaction or interaction patterns, it does appear that Miller and Hamblin's findings for productivity are relevant for those variables as well. A study by Myers (1962) indicated that situation 2 has greater satisfaction than situation 1. Also, the study by Ilgen and

O'Brien (1968) indicated that greater communication took place in collaborative tasks than tasks where individuals were not interdependent.

The implications of these findings are important. Organizations should be careful to match their reward structure with the degree of interdependence inherent in the task. To introduce what is traditionally called a competitive system (high differential reward) when employees are dependent upon each other may very well decrease performance instead of increasing it. To make sure that every one gets the same compensation on a task where employees work and contribute independently may hinder effectiveness. (Scott and Mitchell, 1972, p. 123)

There are some other major implications of these findings, given the nature of complex organizations.

First, individuals don't see themselves as contributing independently, particularly if they are a part of a larger unit. That larger unit is often differentially rewarded for its contribution to the overall nature and functioning of the organization. The unit will be a part of a hierarchical structure and thus will be a part of a competitive process. As such, individuals have been socialized to behave in competitive ways. Competitive ways are not independent ways. By definition, individuals are a part of a larger process if they are to be either winners or losers in the competitive struggle.

Second, organizations don't have the choice of differential reward — it is a given by nature of a hierarchical arrangement. All units, hence all individuals, are not rewarded equally.

Individuals and subsystems then begin to perceive themselves as acting independently, if they gear their perception to the reward system, but they may also see themselves as acting in an interactive fashion in regard to the task, technology, or informal system of communication and interaction. The organization gives mixed messages, but individuals respond primarily to the reward system, so they begin to act in terms of the differential reward system. Once again the competitive process is reinforced in the organizational context.

Hellriegel and Slocum (1974) modify some of Deutsch's (1969a) earlier work to present a summary of the consequences of competitive and cooperative interpersonal relationships (Figure 3-1). Note that the results of competitive interpersonal relationships revolve around antagonism and power minimization; suspicion and hostility; separation of interests and minimization of similarities; and misleading communication and espionage.

Cooperative interpersonal relationships, on the other hand, emphasize mutual interests and power enhancement; trust and responsiveness; sensitivity to common interests and convergence of beliefs; and accurate communication.

Hellriegel and Slocum (1974) also summarize a case study done by Dutton and Walton (1972), which contrasts functioning between sales and production units within two districts of the same organization (Figure 3-2).

This work and analysis is consistent with Deutsch and other behavioral scientists who have collected data and analyzed differences between competitive and cooperative methodologies, value systems, and behavior patterns in organizational settings.

Napier and Gershenfeld (1973) list some of the outcomes which are likely to be found when individuals enter into a task with a predefined need to be cooperative and interdependent. Some of these are:

—more listening;
—more acceptance of ideas;
—less possessiveness of ideas;
—more communication;
—more self-imposed (group) achievement pressure;
—more attentiveness to member's ideas; and
—a friendly climate.

Three conditions are necessary for cooperation in organizational settings. There are: (1) internal social stability within each unit, (2) external value sharing between parties, that is, awareness of interdependence and agreement on the values and objectives of the larger unit of which they are a part; and (3) a legitimate authority hierarchy, with both parties agreeing to relative status, authority, and interaction flow (Dalton, 1963).

These conditions are seldom met in today's organizations. First, internal social stability is inconsistent with the nature of hierarchy, the resultant competition, and the striving for upward mobility as a precondition for minimal movement and maintenance within the system. This condition is most often evident in its impact on individual behavior. The nature of hierarchy has at its core the preservation and perpetuation of stability, but competition results in a continual reshuffling and rearrangement of power and control as individuals vie for a perceived larger share of what is seen as a fixed "power pie." (See Chapter 8 for more detailed focus on "power pie.") The first condition of social stability, then, is not met because of the nature of the organization.

Second, the condition of external value sharing may very often be met, but the problem arises with the way in which this criterion is met. The commonly shared value system is consistent with a competitive mentality. It is a value system that is inconsistent, in fact even mutually exclusive, with the value system implicit in a cooperative situation. Thus, even if units agree on interdependence in terms of task and agree on common outcomes in terms of the task, there is still the implicit agreement on competitive values and the subsequent struggle over some perceived scarcity of resources.

Third, there is often agreement on a legitimate authority hierarchy; however, individuals are seldom willing (or rewarded, for that matter) to maintain a relative amount of status, authority, or interaction. Acceptance of that relativity

Figure 3-1 Consequences of Cooperative versus Competitive Interpersonal Relationships[1]

Dimension	Relationship	
	Competitive	*Cooperative*
Task Orientation	Emphasis on antagonistic interests; the minimization of the other's power becomes an objective.	Highlighting of mutual interests, coordinated effort with division of labor and specialization of function; substitutability of effort rather than duplication; the enhancement of mutual power becomes an objective.
Attitudes	Suspicious, hostile attitudes with a readiness to exploit the other's needs and weakness and a negative responsiveness to the other's requests.	Trusting, friendly attitudes with a positive interest in the other's welfare and a readiness to respond helpfully to the other's needs and requests.
Perception	Increased sensitivity to opposed interests, to threats, and to minimizing the awareness of similarities.	Increased sensitivity to common interests while minimizing the salience of opposed interests; a sense of convergence of beliefs and values.

| Communication | Little communication or misleading communication; espionage or other techniques to obtain information the other is willing to give; each seeks to obtain accurate information about the other but to mislead, discourage, or intimidate the other, coercive tactics are employed. | Open, honest communication of relevant information; each is interested in accurately informing as well as being informed; communication is persuasive rather than coercive in intent. |

[1]M. Deutsch, "Socially Relevant Science: Reflections on Some Studies of Interpersonal Conflict," American Psychologist, 1969, 24, p. 1078. In Hellriegel, D. & Slocum, J. W. *Management: A Contingency Approach.* Reading, Massachusetts, Addison-Wesley, 1974, p. 404.

Figure 3-2   Two Approaches to Interunit Relationships[2]

Dimensions	Win-Lose Orientation	Collaborative Orientation
1. Goals and orientation to decision making	1. Each unit emphasized the requirements of its own particular task.	1. Each unit stressed common goals whenever possible and in other cases tried to balance goals.
2. Information handling	2. Each unit (a) minimized the other's problems or tended to ignore them when recognized and (b) minimized or distorted the information communicated.	2. Each unit tried to understand the other's problems and give consideration to them and (b) tried to provide the other with full, timely, and accurate information relevant to joint decisions.
3. Freedom of movement	3. Each unit tried to gain maximum freedom for itself and to limit the freedom for the other through such tactics as: (a) circumventing formal procedures; (b) emphasizing jurisdictional rules; (c) trying to fix the future performance obligations of the other unit; (d) restricting interaction patterns; (e) pressure tactics such as hierarchical appeals; (f) blaming the other for past failures in performance.	3. Each unit tried to increase its freedom to attain goals through the following actions: (a) accepting informal procedures which facilitated task achievement; (b) blurring of the differences between production and sales; (c) avoiding trying to fix the unit's future performance; (d) encouraging relatively open interaction patterns; (e) searching for solutions rather than employing pressure tactics; (f) focusing on the diagnosis and correction of defects in rules rather than placing blame.

4. Attitudes

4. Each unit developed negative feelings toward the other. Desires to threaten, vent hostilities, and retaliate were common.

4. Each unit adopted trusting and positive attitudes toward the other.

---

[2] Abridged from J.M. Dutton & R.E. Walton, "Interdepartmental Conflict and Cooperation: Two Contrasting Studies. In Hellriegal, D., and Slocum, J.W. *Management: A Contingency Approach.* Reading, Mass.: Addison-Wesley, 1974, p. 395.

would be counter to the larger rules of the game of corporate mobility and power enlargement. Organizations reward employees for striving, *not* maintaining; for growth, *not* stability; for increases, *not* maintenance. Once again, this condition is seldom met, given the nature of a hierarchy and the competitive set of organizational structures, processes, and reward systems.

Consequently, the conditions necessary for cooperation to flourish are extremely unlikely in organizational settings due to their heavily rewarded hierarchical and competitive mechanisms.

There are some internal dynamics in organizations that facilitate some movement toward a collaborative framework:

> For the organization to act as a unity, we need integration or collaboration among the various departments. Thus, management frequently faces a problem: long-run performance requires substantial integration, but efforts to generate collaboration often produce short run conflict. It is often easier simply to allow differentiation to dominate over integration. (Hampton, Summer, and Webber, 1973, p. 672)

Part of the reason for this short-run conflict emerges because collaborative structures and processes are inconsistent with the more potent but often implicit values and processes that support and reward competition.

People do things because there is something in it for them. That something has to do with more long range rewards and expectations built around defined appropriate behavior in an organizational context. Just as managers are not likely to be very enthusiastic about collaborative processes, subordinates are likely to be even less enthusiastic. Even if a manager has some vague notions and makes some veiled suggestions that a particular collaborative methodology or behavior pattern is appropriate for a given situation or task, there is little to suggest that this will be regarded as appropriate by a given group of subordinates. They are most likely to see this in a broader historical context of what "usually" happens in this unit and not to be particularly responsive to its adoption. In fact, they are more likely to resist covertly if not overtly. The employees see the manager as out of touch with the "real" functioning of the organization, as "soft," and perhaps not someone who is capable of, or likely to be, acting in their best interests.

The manager who suggests a collaborative or integrative perspective or methodology to a superior is likely to be considered "incapable of handling the rigors of organizational life." He/she is subtly perceived as not understanding what it takes to get the job done, or as someone who is not "results oriented." Indeed, all are likely outcomes that make the move towards a collaborative framework vastly complicated.

The utilization of shared decision-making and power equalization is an important part of a collaborative orientation. Neither is likely to emerge out of a wish or a desire on the part of one manager alone.

There are some very real dangers and opportunities for disillusionment on the part of groups and organizations if these methodologies are entered into lightly or without a clear realization of some of the restraints.

> To have a large group (or organization) involved in a decision-making process when, in fact, only a few individuals have the power to control what actually happens can lead to disillusionment and resistance among those who detect their own impotence. Credibility will become even more strained if those with power are perceived as being inflexible and using the elaborate problem-solving procedures to help them look as if they are open to new ideas. If there is no accountability and responsibility built into the group, if real decisions are made behind the scenes, then the work sessions of the larger group (organizations) will be reduced to a climate of relative indifference over the major issues, and energy will be channeled into secondary issues with less powerful individuals

attempting to assert themselves. (Napier and Gershenfeld, 1973, p. 201)

Disillusionment and resistance are natural outgrowths of a hierarchical model. Vertical differentiation is a core of a hierarchy, which leads to responsibility (ultimate responsibility) being placed higher and higher in the organization. This upward push is accompanied by clarified expectations that involvement and investment are not appropriate responses for individuals. What is seen as appropriate is an enlarged commitment to the authority hierarchy and power grabbing. Power gathering rather than power equalization result. Power is seen as the end in itself. Being a good "organizational person" becomes the ultimate aim. As Bogart and Tipps (1973) have so succinctly stated, "Species O," or the organizational mentality, is clearly with us, alive and well in organizations and social systems. Species O is present when the organization takes the place of the individual, when the structures and processes rule the individual instead of the reverse.

Competition has serious and predictable outcomes in terms of behavior patterns of individuals. Walton (1970) has delineated some behaviors that are "effective" in competitive and collaborative settings:

Effective Competitive Behavior	*Effective Collaborative Behavior*
1. Behavior is directed toward achieving personal goals.	1. Behavior is directed toward achieving goals held in common.
2. Secrecy	2. Openness.
3. Our needs are hidden or misrepresented even though accurately understood. This means others don't know how much you will give up since they don't know exactly what you want.	3. Accurate representation of clearly understood, personal needs.

4. Use of surprise and un-predictability as well as mixed strategies.

5. Bluffs and threats

6. Logical, nonrational and irrational arguments are used to defend a position to which you are strategically committed.

7. Where teams, committees, or organizations are involved, communicaing bad stereotypes of the other, ignoring his logic, and arousing in-group hostility. This tends to strengthen in-group loyalty, increase motivation, and convince others you mean business.

4. Predictability/flexibility is utilized, but not as a surprise tactic.

5. Bluffs and threats are not used.

6. Logical and innovative processes are used to defend your views, if you are convinced of their validity, or to find solutions to problems.

7. Success demands that stereotypes be dropped, that ideas be given consideration on their merit regardless of sources, and that good working relationships be maintained. Positive feelings about others are both a cause and an effect of collaboration.

When one reads the list of competitive strategies, feelings of distress, fear, depression, and some feelings of incredulity emerge. "How could this possibly be true?" one asks. Yet stopping for a moment and thinking about life and behavior in organizations reveals these strategies to be fairly commonplace. On the cold printed page they stand out, but within organizational life they blend with the other behavior patterns that are very much like them. Indeed, when the list of behaviors in the collaborative column are examined, the realization becomes obvious that these are the behaviors that seem to be viewed by others as out of place in terms of organizational life on a continuing basis.

Kolb, Rubin, and McIntyre (1974)[1] do a nice job of summarizing three of the consequences of utilizing competitive strategies. They are:

[1] These outcomes are also similar to Deutsch's (1973) review of competitive processes.

1. The development of a competitive, win-lose climate that emphasizes the separateness of "we" and "they" and feelings that "we" are superior and "they" are inferior. Individual factions or groups under competitive pressure invariably rate themselves above-average in both cohesion and ability.
2. Distortions in judgment. Individuals or groups under competitive pressure invariably evaluate their own contributions as best, and fall into downgrading efforts of others.
3. Distortions in perception. Experiments demonstrate that under competitive pressure persons perceive that they understand the other person's proposal when in fact they do not. Consequently, areas shared in common are likely to go unrecognized. (p. 190)

In summary, then, cooperative groups exhibit the following characteristics:

1. More effective intermember communcication;
2. More friendliness, more helpfulness, less obstructiveness;
3. More coordination, more division of labor, more orientation to task achievement, more orderliness in discussion, higher productivity; and
4. More feeling of agreement and similiarity of ideas, more confidence in one's own ideas and in the value others attach to these ideas. (Deutsch, 1973)

These outcomes are also supported by a variety of other authors (Back, 1951; Mintz, 1951; Mizuhara and Tamai, 1952; Gerard, 1953; Levy, 1953; Grossack, 1954; Margolin, 1954; Gottheil, 1955; Berkowitz, 1957; Thomas, 1957; Raven and Eachus, 1963; and Workie, 1967).

Thayer (1973) focuses on the possibility that to *"tie wages to productivity, and perhaps to tie income to em-*

ployment, is to perpetuate alienation" (p. 36). He goes on to discuss the conventional view that workers are many times only extensions of technology or merely a *thing.*

A French sociologist, Ellul (1964) argues that phenomena originally designed for the benefit of the individual eventually end up engulfing the individual.

> Even when we speak of adapting the machine or the organization to the individual, we forgot that adaption is inevitably reciprocal; hence the individual adapts to the organization, and it swallows him. Over time, so goes the Ellulian argument, the *means* (organization) consumes those for whom it was designed to achieve an *end.* (Thayer, 1973, p. 48)

> Universities are additional organizations which emphasize competition in terms of the processes of functioning. Intellectuals pride themselves on the "collegial" or "family" relationships they enjoy as supposedly self actualized individuals. At the same time, they raise higher walls between academic disciplines, argue that "facts" can objectively be separated from values, insist that knowledge can be made certain, and retain the right, by virtue of their "knowledge" to impose their views upon students or junior colleagues seeking tenure—thereby acting out roles indistinguishable from those in other superior-subordinate relationships. (Thayer, 1973), p. 51

This *reciprocity of interaction* to which both Ellul and Thayer allude is at the core of the interaction of the individual and the organizational context within which he/she finds himself/herself.

Socialization leads to competitive values, and competitive behavior is reinforced by the organization in the form of hierarchy, and finally seen as the only "reasonable" way to behave by individuals who function in that setting. The university, in all its infinite rhetoric, is probably the clearest example of this reciprocity of interaction. Its inconsistencies between rhetoric and action clearly exemplify the reciprocity of hierarchy and competition.

In short, managerial controls tend to create group rivalries, force groups to think of their own and not other's problems, reward an overall point of view rarely, and place groups in win-lose situations in which they are competing with each other for the scarce resources. (Argyris, 1970, pp. 61-62)

INDIVIDUAL BALANCE AND REDUCTION OF DISSONANCE

Leon Festinger (1957) has done some of the classic experimentation and formulation of concepts regarding the ways in which individuals resolve seemingly irresolvable or irreconcilable positions. Individuals are quite adept at a process called cognitive dissonance: they will rationalize a perspective that makes it possible for them to see a way for two seemingly conflicting situations to appear to have a reconcilable "fit." This dynamic provides some explanation for why individuals can function in organizational settings that supposedly stand for teamwork, interdependence, and goal congruence. They simply force a "fit" for those pieces that, from other perspectives, really don't go together.

Chris Argyris (1969, 1970) has suggested that social psychological theory and research indicate social interaction process tendencies toward: (1) consistency or balance (or reduction of dissonance); (2) attribution; and (3) evaluation. Argyris (1970; Argyris and Schon, 1978) identified two composite behavior patterns that he labeled Pattern A and Pattern B. Pattern A behavior composite would include:

—little expression of feelings;
—little experimenting;
—little risk-taking;
—little helping of others to own their own ideas and feelings;
—little openness and experimentation;

—few norms of trust; or

—little concern for feelings.

Pattern B behavior would be composed of the following:

—rewards for the expression of feelings;

—rewards for the helping of others;

—rewards for taking risks; and

—strong norms or trust, concern, and individuality.

Argyris goes on to say that Pattern A behaviors are the typical ones in most organizational contexts. He further states that most individuals are unaware of their behavior patterns, that they espouse a conceptual framework that, if used, would be consistent with Pattern B behaviors. Their actual behaviors, however, are most closely aligned with Pattern A. Even when confronted with this discrepancy between espoused and actual behavior, they are seldom able to change behaviors without a great deal of effort and training.

This apparent inconsistency is, in fact, consistent with the hypothesis about dissonance reduction in individuals. This is also helpful in further understanding some of the process of adaptation that is involved for individuals and social systems in terms of the reciprocity of interaction previously mentioned.

Individuals and organizations often espouse a theory of cooperation and mutual interdependence and interaction. They claim that their methodologies, values, and behaviors are consistent with a collaborative model. Even when confronted with possible discrepancies, they are hard-pressed to see these discrepancies clearly. Their behaviors around competition and the accompanying structure of hierarchy are in fact consistent with each other. They are inconsistent with the model of cooperation and mutual task interdependence.

Both superiors and subordinates are a part of the process. The hierarchy of authority is clearly in place with little ability to examine clearly the impact of that placement. The handmaiden of hierarchy, competition, is also clearly in place and continues to survive elegantly.

> The ruled, for their part, cannot dispense with or replace the bureaucratic apparatus of authority once it exists. For this bureaucracy rests upon expert training (socialization), a functional specialization of work, and an attitude set for habitual and virtuoso-like mastery of single yet methodically integrated functions. (Weber, 1946, p. 37)

HIERARCHY

What keeps competition alive and well in organizations? Some of the ways in which competition is reinforced by hierarchy have been examined.

In addition to the reciprocity of interaction between competition and hierarchy, hierarchy continues to flourish for other reasons.

> Men are eager to be "bossed" by superior ability, but they resent being bossed by men of no greater ability than they themselves have. So strong is this need of assigning superior status to those in positions of command that, unless the obvious facts preclude it, men will impute abilities they cannot recognize or judge. They want to believe that those of higher authority "know what they are doing. . . ." This desire for the justification of subordination leads often to profuse rationalization about status and even to mythological and mystical explanation of it. (Barnard, 1946, pp. 60-61)

Although this was written more than 30 years ago, it still describes the interaction of status and hierarchy in the current organization.

Status and the perpetuation of status as a discriminating dynamic feeds the hierarchy of authority. Individuals are again caught in a process where they find themselves supporting hierarchy as a means to preserve some individuality and also perpetuating the competitive mechanisms as a game that has familiar rules. This allows them to have easier access to some status and imparts a feeling of control or influence over their organizational life.

As C. Wright Mills has so eloquently stated:

> In the white-collar hierarchies, individuals are often segregated by minute gradations of rank and, at the same time, subject to a fragmentation of skill. This bureaucratization often breaks up the occupational basis of their prestige. Since the individual may seize upon minute distinctions on the basis of status, these distinctions operate against any status solidarity among the mass of employees, often lead to status estrangement from work associates, and to increased status competition . . . Above all, the hierarchy is often accompanied by a delirium for status merely because of its authoritarian shape: as Karl Manheim has observed, people who are dependent for everything, including images of themselves, upon place in an authoritarian hierarchy, will all the more frantically cling to claims of status. (1951, pp. 254-255)

Americans have a tremendous penchant for authority. There is a tremendous resistance to rejection of authority as demonstrated in a very frightening series of experiments by Milgram (1974).

Milgram's subjects were told that they were involved in an experiment to test the effects of punitive stimuli on learning. They were informed that their task was to give a series of shocks to subjects strapped to a chair in an adjoining room whenever the subjects made a mistake. The strength of the shocks was to be progressively increased for each mistake. The highest voltages were labeled as "dangerous," the range being from 15 to 440 volts.

Sixty-two percent of the subjects obeyed the instructors, even though simulated cries of pain could be heard from the other room. Individuals laughed hysterically and indicated they would not take responsibility, but at the instructors' insistence, they continued to administer the shock. The experiment indicates that dispositions to obey authority are strong in individuals.

Milgram (1974) indicates that anxiety is generated when respondents are forced to reject authority. The anxiety arises

> from the individual's long history of socialization. He (she) has, in the course of moving from a biological creature to a civilized person, internalized the basic rules of social life. And the most basic of these is respect for authority. The rules are internally enforced by linking their possible breach to a flow of disruptive, ego-threatening affect. The emotional signs observed in the laboratory — trembling, anxious laughter, acute embarrassment — are evidence of an assault on these rules. As the subject comtemplates this break, anxiety is generated, signaling him (her) to step back from the forbidden action and thereby creating an emotional barrier through which he (she) must pass in order to defy authority. (p. 152)

Some experimental evidence for the movement of conflict from a political issue to one that also has a biological base is apparent. The socialization of individuals is consistent with the behavior pattern of competition emerging from this situation. A strong dependency on the hierarchy of authority almost as a crutch to dictate behavior is indicated. It is consistent with socialization, and it leaves a great deal of anxiety and a somewhat less well-defined feeling of alienation.

HIERARCHY, WORK, AND ALIENATION

One of the outcomes of a hierarchical structure seems to be a competitive behavior pattern on the part of individuals. A concommitant result is some form of alienation, or at least some feelings of distance from influence over life in a particular organizational setting. There are trade-offs for this distance. As Presthus (1978) states:

> The status system enhances motivation and discipline by its promise of highly valued rewards and its immediate psychic income. As the displacement of value from work to its by-products has eroded the almost uniquely American emphasis upon achievement, status, and prestige have become more highly valued in themselves. (p. 134)

Research data regarding the relationship between alienation and investment and organizational structure are not consistent.

There seems to be a curvilinear relationship between technology and alienation and satisfaction with the work itself. Alienation seems to be lowest for individuals in a craft technology, highest for individuals in assembly line technologies, and medium for individuals in a machine-tending technology (Blauner, 1964; Herbert, 1976)

David Payne (1974) further suggests that alienation from work is not related to alienation from a larger society, nor are feelings of powerlessness related to the type of work. Another study concludes that in a

> large-scale, capitalist system, control over the product of one's labor, ownership and hierarchical position has only an indirect effect on alienation, whereas control over work process (closeness of supervision, routination, and substantive complexity) has an appreciable direct effect on powerlessness, self-estrangement, and normlessness (Kohn, 1976, p. 111).

While this study may not explicitly support the notion of hierarchy and its ensuing alienation, there is some indirect support in that the variables that do lead to powerlessness are direct results of a hierarchical model.

Routinization and complexity are processes that are

directly influenced by the degree of hierarchical control and the degree of reinforced competitive behavior within the organizational setting.

Organizations are designed to make individuals (members) interchangeable parts. They are designed to insure substitution of membership.

Individuals contribute to this perpetuation when they demand clear job descriptions and clear lines of career development. This clarification increases the probability that a higher percentage of individuals who can do the same job in similar fashion can easily be found.

It also makes it easier for individuals to play the "game" of competition, as they vie to establish some unique chacteristics in a system designed to keep them the same, or at least not significantly different from other members of the social system. *Conformity with distinction* becomes the byword for life and functioning in the organization. Any characteristic or behavior or value that is "too" different from the mainstream of the expectations of the organization is seen as being deviant. The deviant person is subsequently punished by not being allowed to play the game of continuation in the organization. Individuals soon learn that conformity is the only appropriate response. They are just not willing to pay the costs of resisting primary organizational norms of competition for status, power, and control. Their response is often something like "It's not a very good game, and I don't really care for it, but after all it's the only game in town."

Thompson (1967) has argued that technology is the major independent variable leading to the development of hierarchy. He acknowledges that authority exists but does not link it directly with hierarchy. He goes on to say that it is unfortunate that hierarchy has come to mean "higher" and "lower," implying that it doesn't have to be that way.

I strongly disagree! The nature of the concept has as a central precept the notion of greater and lesser. This surely is a short jump to higher and lower. What may have started out as a simple breakdown of functions has become an end in itself.

Vertical differentiation is a core component of hierarchy — in fact it is *the* core component. As long as this remains a central tendency in organizational structure, design, and functioning, a hierarchy of authority will exist along with it and the accompanying values system and behavior pattern of competition will continue.

MARKETING AND UNDERWRITING: AN EXAMPLE

While maintaining that all organizations in Western society are hierarchically organized, the use of an example from an insurance company is not meant to imply that this type of organization is any more (or less) hierarchically oriented than a variety of others that could be examined.

Underwriters in an insurance company are responsible for assessing the risk involved in accepting a given policy. They have a major voice in determining whether or not a policy is accepted. Essentially they are rewarded, indirectly of course, for turning down policies. The end result is that they have the responsibility for "not accepting" potential business for the organization. They are rewarded partially according to how much business they turn away. In fact, they are expected to turn away a certain percentage of customers on the basis that the risk is too great, the percentage varying from company to company. Part of their reward is based on profitability, not necessarily production, per se.

Marketing people, on the other hand, are rewarded primarily for production. They are expected to sell and are rewarded for "selling" policies. They are not expected to assess risk. That is someone else's job in the organization. Marketing personnel expect to be rewarded accordingly if their sales climb.

The situation has been somewhat exaggerated in order

to make a point, but the primary dynamics are as described.

What happens when these two "types" begin to look at their behavior and value system in terms of the larger organization, of which they are both members. They are both told (by their respective managers) that they and the functions that they perform are vital for the continuation of the organization. They are informed that the life of the organization could be crippled if their functions were not continued and continued at an even more vigorous level than previously.

They begin to see themselves as important in the life of the organization. They begin to see that it is important to have resources in order to accomplish their tasks in vigorous ways. They look around the organization and quickly determine that the only way to accomplish this is to compete with someone else. They soon discover that the way to the resources is control, authority, and influence. It becomes clear that the resources of status and prestige are largely perceptual in nature, in that getting others to "believe" that you are influential is essential.

They begin to use the competitive process to accumulate a series of "wins," to be tagged a "winner." They begin to set up conditions where the other person begins to look like a "loser." If all else fails, it is appropriate to make sure that they don't lose any of the competitive edge they may have developed thus far in the organization.

It becomes a game of lose-lose, or making sure that if you can't win, at least you won't lose anything. This is complicated when both parties arrive at this conclusion at the same time.

So the competition that began as a *facilitating* strategy has quickly become a *maintaining* strategy for individuals and for the organization in general. It certainly has not done anything for the original goals of increased production and profitability with which the various units were struggling. Both parties have learned the appropriate behavior patterns, and these patterns are appropriate for the situation in which they find themselves.

SALES AND SERVICE: ANOTHER EXAMPLE

Another example of competition between units and individuals created and maintained by a hierarchical organizational structure is the conflict between sales and service departments. This conflict is probably at its highest in those organizations that sell a variety of products, each of which needs some tailoring to a particular client's needs, and for which a systematic diagnosis of client needs is performed prior to deciding which specific model of a product line is to be sold.

This systematic analysis is often performed by the sales person. He/she is rewarded with a higher rate for some products than for others. He/she may be under some pressure to sell more or less of a particular product. At any rate, all the products do not have an equal probability of being sold, from an organizational perspective.

The service person must respond to these products after they have been sold. This person is indirectly rewarded for finding problems with what the sales person has done. He/she must have some problems to which to respond, so if there aren't any, "we'll just have to create some."

Again, the same series of dynamics is likely to emerge. The two individuals and the two units are rewarded for different types of behavior. They are almost forced to engage in a competitive behavior pattern, in which someone is very likely to become the "loser," or very adept at playing the "lose-lose" game.

An inherent tension emerges within the framework where these two units function. Each is reluctant to name the game — in fact, each begins to reduce the dissonance by supporting it and becoming quite an able player.

Indeed, Weber (1968) was quite succinct when he observed that, "In a modern state the actual ruler is necessarily and unavoidably the bureaucracy." (p. 1393).

The next chapter examines in more detail the forces which facilitate the continuation of a hierarchical model, and also looks at some of the forces that push forward toward a collaborative perspective.

Chapter 4

FORCES PERPETUATING COMPETITION AND PUSHING FOR COLLABORATION

It is a bit ludicrous to attempt to delineate in one chapter the forces perpetuating competition. It is appropriate to spend some time on those forces, yet it is difficult to specify clearly all of the elements that reinforce this behavior pattern. Some of the forces have been discussed in the preceding chapter by examining how organizations have been set up to foster and reward behavior patterns and value systems consistent with this methodology.

In a sense, then, this chapter will pull together some of the threads that foster competition. In addition, it will examine some of the dynamics observed in school systems since they are major cultural perpetuators in this society. Research will continue to focus on some of the values inherent in a competitive system, since it has already been stated that these values foster the continuation of the present system of organizational structuring and functioning.

Power is also reexamined as it is ingrained in the forces that perpetuate competition. Power will be discussed in more detail in Chapter 8, as it ties in with competitive systems, and how it appears in a collaborative organizational system.

This chapter also examines some of the forces in the United States as well as in Europe that are pushing us to seek alternatives to competitive and hierarchical systems.

FORCES PERPETUATING COMPETITION

Organizations are political structures, which embrace authority distribution systems and processes related to the distribution and exercise of power. Power should be understood as a relationship; part of that relationship emerges from the perception by one party that power is in the possession of another. If one perceives a scarcity on his/her part (by definition this implies he/she wants more), then he/she is likely to pursue processes that will increase his/her share of power.

Competition exists primarily in an economy of scarcity — particularly a scarcity of power — as defined by the parameters of hierarchical structure. This power scarcity arises under two sets of conditions:

1. Where individuals gain power in absolute terms at someone else's expense and
2. Where there is a comparative gain that results in a relative shift in the distribution of power. This shift is, not literally at someone else's expense. (Zaleznik, 1973, p. 716)

Zaleznik explains this behavior in terms of a psychology of scarcity as well as a process of social comparisons.

> The human being tends to make comparisons as a basis for his sense of self esteem. He may compare himself with other

people and decide that his absolute loss or the shift in proportional shares of authority reflects an attrition in his power base. He may also compare his position relative to others against a personal standard and feel a sense of loss. This tendency to compare is deeply ingrained in people, especially since they experience early in life the effects of comparisons in the family where — in an absolute sense — time and and attention, if not love and affection, go to the most dependent member. (1973, p. 716)

Zaleznik (1973) and Ingalls (1976) further describe the nature of organizations as pyramids, which result in a scarcity of positions as one moves up the hierarchical ladder. Zaleznik presents a rationale for competition as a mainstay in organizational life and function, saying:

It may be humane and socially desirable to say that people are different rather than unequal in their potential, nevertheless executive talent is in short supply. The end result should be to move the more able people into the top positions and to accord them the pay, responsibility, and authority to match their potential. (p. 716)

Using the pyramid to predict competition for scarce resources (positions), Zalenzik then uses competition to justify the need for the pyramidal structure. It is this type of circular reasoning that continues to encourage the perception of competition as a given and an independent variable rather than a dependent variable in organizational functioning.

There is a propensity in all of the organizational literature and in individual perspectives to see competition as necessary rather than as a process, which is used to explain the need for its continuation. This parallels the propensity for consistency in our views of organizational life. It is also consistent with a need for dissonance reduction in the culture and in the social systems that comprise the culture

—those with which we identify to determine who we are, what we should value, and how we should behave.

Organizational theorists frequently perpetuate the inherent goodness, or at least the inevitability, of competition in organizational life. There is generated an implicit feeling that to question this is to confront the core of all that is true in the world (at least the world as we know it in our perceptual framework).

Locke (1968) offers a very clear example of this propensity toward blind loyalty to competition with little examination of its side effects or little awareness of its impact on perpetuation of values and structures that do not result in the originally intended outcomes. Locke (1968) states:

> It is well known, both from experimental studies and from everyday experience, that competition can serve as an incentive to increase one's effort on a task. This phenomenon is an intrinsic part of athletics and business and is not unknown in academia. In the paradigm case of competition, another person's or group's performance is the standard by which goals are set and success and failure judged. One reason competition in athletics is so effective is that winning requires that one surpass the performance of the best existing competitor. This typically results in the standard of success becoming progressively more difficult with time. Each time a record is broken, the level of performance required to win (against the record holder) is raised. Each competitior must then readjust his goals and his level of effort to the difficulty of the task. The result is progressively better performance. (Of course cognitive factors can facilitate performance improvement, i.e., discovering better methods of performing the task. But it is the individual's goal to win or improve that generally motivates the search for such innovations.)
>
> The case is similar though not identical in business (unlike athletics, business is not a "zero-sum game," where one man's gain necessarily means another man's loss. In business, wealth is created and therefore everyone benefits in the long run.) Competition will encourage the development of better and better products as long as there are firms who wish to increase their share of the market. Competition may

also spur firms to increase their quality or lower prices in order not to lose business.

The effect of competition, both between individuals and between groups, depends upon the particular person or persons one is competing with and one's own values. In athletics, the goal is typically to beat the best other competitor. In business this is not always the case; typically, business firms are satisfied to surpass their own best previous performances: Students if they are competing will ordinarily pick other students with grades or abilities similar to their own to compete with, or else will try to surpass their own best previous grade-point average.

The case of an individual trying to improve over his own previous performance on a task can be considered a special case of competition: self-competition.

As with participation, competition may have other effects besides inducing goal-setting. Above all, competition probably encourages individuals to remain committed to goals that they might otherwise abandon in the face of fatigue and difficulty. For instance, if mile runners only ran against themselves or against a stop watch, the 4-minute mile might never have been broken.

In addition, competition encourages the setting of goals that might not have been set at all in the absence of the other party. For example, if the Ford Motor Company had not developed a mass-produced low-priced automobile, General Motors might not have thought of developing a similar (competing) model (at that particular time). (pp. 238-39)

Several myths abound in this excerpt. It is a clear example of "Truth, Justice, and the American Way," with little examination of the impact of these value systems on individual and organizational behavior. Some of these myths include:

1. *Businesses are like athletics.* There is some similarity between an athletic contest and the *actual* behavior pattern that emerges in an organizational context. Perhaps what is important here is the degree to which the value systems and expected behavior patterns are "out front"

in athletic competition as opposed to organizations where the expected outcomes are obscured by the rhetoric of cooperation and interdependence.

There are also greater social consequences of the outcomes in organizations than there are in athletics. Many individuals are affected in terms of their careers and their lives, not to mention the additional cost passed on to individuals.

2. *The individual goal to win fosters innovation.* This is just not borne out in organizational life, nor is it in any way consistent with the qualitative and quantitative research literature on organizational behavior. Particularly in the United States, there is little individual innovation in terms of creativity, and certainly not in terms of organizational design and structure. Individuals instead learn how to "play the game" with "style" rather than learning how to question, and rarely change any of the basic rules. Competition just doesn't encourage growth or creativity. It doesn't foster openness or trust or risk-taking, all of which are necessary for creativity and innovation, as well as individual growth and development.

Competition encourages more effective "rule-learning" behavior, not "rule-questioning" behavior. An individual quickly learns how to minimize losses, how to state perspectives in order to appear cooperative or compromising, when in fact the individual is trying to "cover his/her bets." Again, the game cannot be questioned, for part of the game is not to question the game!

3. *Business is a "zero-sum game."* Locke misses the point that organizations *are* structured *as if* existence therein were a "zero-sum game." As people strive for consistency in the world, they begin to behave in ways that are consistent with that structure. A hierarchy cannot be understood in any other way than to see as its major

component a set of structural dynamics and processes that perpetuate this perception.

If there is always someone else who has ultimate responsibility at the same time you are supposed to demonstrate your ability to "take" responsibility and utilize it in the best interests of the organization, what other conclusion can you draw? It might be possible to pull this off, if you are the only individual in this position, but that is rarely the case. Every individual in the organization is in the same situation. Each person is trying to demonstrate his/her competence, and the only way to do that is to do it at someone else's expense. That is an inevitable outcome in a hierarchical structure.

The primary mechanism operating in organizations is *differentiation*. There are departments, functions, job descriptions, grievance procedures, roles, status, titles, promotions, mobility, and hierarchy. Organizations sometimes implement mechanisms of *integration* designed to foster interdependence, but these are often only superficial measures for a particular situation. They seldom become mainstays or primary dynamics of organizational life.

Given these dynamics in organizational life, all must learn to behave in ways that lead closer to organizational rewards in attempt to play the "zero-sum game" that doesn't exist! It is possible to get some clues that behavior is dysfunctional to the accomplishment of the stated organizational goals or to the completion of the organizational goals. But all eventually learn to behave in ways that lead closer to organizational rewards in an attempt to "survive elegantly" or to survive at all since it really is the "only game in town."

4. *One person's gain is not another person's loss.* What happens when one person receives a promotion and another does not? The reality in organizational life is

that the person who has lost a promotion, particularly if he/she loses several, becomes tagged as a "loser." He/she has lost status and prestige, as well as a promotion. One must be very cautious in responding that perhaps it was deserved. Perhaps it was, but the nature of the organization is so structured that the dynamics of "missed opportunities" have a powerful impact on the behavior pattern that results.

Kanter (1977), in *Men and Women of the Corporation*, describes this impact with such candor that it becomes clear that much individual behavior is, unfortunately, consistent with the context within which the individual finds himself/herself.

Some of the dynamics that emerge with regard to intergroup competition between departments have already been noted. They can be seen in the outcomes of budget and hiring processes, as departments move further away from each other as a result of that process. The competitive process, by definition, has winners and losers. Thus, by definition, the gain is at someone else's expense since people are behaving in a way that is rewarded by the organization — which is a behavior pattern consistent with a psychology of scarcity.

5. *Self-competition has no negative components.* Self-competition creates severe stress in individuals. As they polish techniques of doing what they know how to do, they are immune to learning new behavior patterns —those that might engender more growth. Individuals and organizations keep saying competition is good, is good, is good. . . .

6. *People like competition.* This myth explodes, perhaps without conscious recognition, in the excerpt, "competition probably encourages individuals to remain committed to goals that they might otherwise abandon in the face of fatigue or difficulty." Exactly. Competition may well be the first to go.

One learns to remain committed to the process because it is so integral to the organization. The real question is, "Would individuals become committed to more important or more relevant goals if the competitive process were not so firmly entrenched?"

This book is based on the premise that the answer is "yes."

7. *"Competition encourages the setting of goals that might not have been set at all in the absence of the other party."* However, the kinds of goals set result in inaccurate communication and perception to and of the other person or group. They result in energy spent on perpetuating one's own existence at the other's expense. They involve minimizing losses rather than taking creative or innovative strides forward in product development.

The aforementioned myths are all too prevalent in popular thinking about life in organizations. They are a part of the socialization processes in the culture as well as in the major socializing system, our schools. Some of the literature that discusses the school system as a perpetuator of competition and hierarchical thinking will be examined, but first, a further look at authority and its relationship to hierarchy.

AUTHORITY AND HIERARCHY

Authority, as it now exists, does little to serve the individual. It clearly serves the purposes of the organization. It allows for a *degree* of rationality and orderliness. Organizations require people to submit to certain rules and regulations as a trade-off for identity and reduced ambiguity. There is a tremendous fear attached to the unknown as it might relate to alternative organizational structures and processes.

Organizations are not particularly tolerant of low levels of ambiguity. (See Ingalls, 1976, for a more detailed description of these processes.)

As organizational functionaries contemplate shifts in organizational functioning, the results are a bit frightening to them.

Leavitt (1972) points out that if organizations move from one-way communication toward two-way communication, there may be changes in perceived organizational relationships as well as a more accurate transmission of facts. Leavitt further states that:

> Authority, for example, may under ideal conditions of two-way communication cease to serve as a sufficient protection for inadequacy. The dictum that a well-informed citizenry is democracy's protection against autocracy may also be applicable to the well-informed staff or well-informed employee.
>
> And though "democracy" may connote things desirable in government, its connotations for industrial organizations in our society are far from clear (p. 121).

Hummel (1977), in a book, entitled *The Bureaucratic Experience*, presents one of the most compelling reasons for the continued existence of the hierarchy. He supports the perpetuation of an elite in terms of power and status, and studies the need to perpetuate a role that has come to have a permanent place in contemporary Western organizations: *the manager.*

> The division of labor, for example, has two purposes. On the one hand, it makes a functionary capable of developing highly specialized skills. The advantage of this may be that the bureaucracy can bring to bear on a specific problem an individual who has the ideal capabilities to resolve that problem. It makes possible the development of the expert. On the other hand, exactly because of that specialization, it is often impossible for one expert to solve the overall problem without the cooperation of other experts. But for this purpose of mobilizing cooperation we need the manager. (p. 30)

What we are now examining is the arrangement of a bureaucracy, which has built into it, because of its hierarchical arrangement, the need for a manager, an overall coordinator, or an integrating mechanism. And yet, the manager whose original function it was to coordinate, not necessarily to "tell' the experts what to do, soon becomes caught in the very dynamics he/she is there to mitigate — namely the competitive struggle for a perceived scarcity of status and organizational rewards in the form of increased power and control so that the system can continue to function with no questions asked.

"People's work is divided, not only to make them expert and more efficient, but to make them dependent on managerial control" (Hummel, 1977, p. 30)

It becomes very difficult to function outside the system. The organization has survival at its core, and Hummel once again comes to the rescue with the proper advice.

> If you want to survive as a bureaucrat, you will never forget that the prime relationship in which you engage is that between you and your manager, not that between you and your client. And that functionary-manager relationship is a control relationship. The successful manager never forgets this. (Hummel, 1977, p. 30)

I do not wish to imply that I am making fun of Hummel or accusing him of giving bad advice. Quite the contrary. Given the nature of current organizational structures and processes, his advice is quite sound. This advice to protect and support the manager is indeed appropriate for the person who wishes to survive elegantly in a contemporary organizational context. It does not, however, do anything to change the nature of the system. Since the *reputation* of individuals in the organization, rather than the job, is often at stake in their everyday interactions, being extremely conscious of authority and the hierarchy of authority in hierarchical organizations is quite a rational response.

The manager's role as developed and refined in Western

organizations has the direct effect of perpetuating the organization, which created and reinforces the role of manager.
The superior in this relationship prospers (although he/she
is also a subordinate in another relationship), but the under-
ling does not fare as well. Tocqueville described this process
in his analysis of American democracy in 1835.

> If proportion as the principle of the division of labor is more
> extensively applied, the workman becomes more weak, more
> narrow-minded, and more dependent. The art advances, the
> artisan recedes. (Tocqueville, 1945 translation, p. 79)

Of course the probable solution to this situation is to
disguise the "real" processes behind the rhetoric of concern,
caring, and harmony.

> Let them believe that they are always in control,
> though it is you who really controls.
> There is no subjugation so perfect
> as that which keeps the appearance of freedom,
> for in that way one captures volition itself.
>
> (Jean-Jacques Rousseau)

Since individuals are likely to strive to perceive consistency in the organizational situation rather than inconsistency, this strategy works rather well. There are even organizational theorists who are able to find support for the
continuation of these processes. Blau (1961) describes the
way individuals perceive these processes when he says:

> To be sure, the status distinctions inherent in the exercise of
> authority are necessary for the effective administration of a
> large organization, where officials in central positions must
> be able to direct and coordinate the work of specialized
> groups. However, since bureaucratic authority rests on social
> consensus that issuing certain directives is just as much the
> duty of the superior as compliance with these directives is that
> of subordinates, such compliance is not experienced as sub-

jugation, while obedience to arbitrary commands of a superior would be. (p. 348)

And further:

> The important point about organizational behavior is that
> the hierarchical structure permits all decisions, except those
> defining ultimate objectives, to rest on factual rather than on
> value premises. (Blau & Scott, 1962, p. 37)

There seems to be some clear implication in Blau's
perspective that people in positions of authority rarely make
arbitrary decisions. That is inconsistent with the nature of a
hierarchy, which rests on those decisions made at each
higher level in the hierarchy based on the role and perspective of the person filling that role.

This borders on being an arbitrary decision if the nature
of the authority hierarchy, the need for the superior to maintain his/her relative power position, and the need to survive
elegantly in a competitive environment that fosters a win-
lose mentality are considered.

It may not be "arbitrary" from the superior's perspective, in fact, he/she may consider it a very pragmatic decision. From the point of view of the subordinate, over the
"long haul," it cannot help but be considered as an arbitrary
decision.

> Every bureaucracy seeks to increase the superiority of the
> professionally informed by keeping their knowledge and in-
> tentions secret. Bureaucratic [hierarchical] administration
> always tends to be an administration of "secret sessions":
> so far as it can, it hides its knowledge and action from criti-
> cism. (Weber, 1946, p. 38)

The perpetuation of the current system is in the best
interests of those who currently hold power in it. Those who
have power are not going to give it up at their own expense
since "control of the status-distribution system gives elites a

powerful sanction, providing compelling incentives for many of its members" (Presthus, 1978, p. 134).

WORKER PARTICIPATION

Haddad (1975) has delineated four levels of worker participation in organizational settings. From most to least involvement these levels are:

Level D: Employee ownership
Level C: Co-determination (co-governance)
Level B: Surface participation in management
Level A: Monetary inclusion

She indicates that very few efforts are really any more than Level B efforts. The social, psychological, political, and economic realities of this country have to this point not led to any real involvement on the part of the vast number of workers in the nature of the organization.

Some countries in Europe have made attempts at worker involvement. Yugoslavia has a heavy focus on worker involvement, but the models adopted there still foster competition. The market strategies, organizational values, and use of hierarchy still remain and, in fact, are stronger than ever. There is merely a different group of individuals at the center and top of the hierarchy (Thayer, 1973).

IS COMPETITION INEVITABLE?

Margulies and Wallace (1973) indicate that:

Realistic competition and open conflict are not necessarily detrimental to organizational behavior. The problems begin when distortions arise that affect the attitudes and behavior of group members in relation to those of some other group. Groups do and must conflict over the distribution of resources; the distribution of information, wealth, power, and status may produce discrepancies which in turn lead to conflict. Groups can, however, learn that conflicts can be settled in productive rather than destructive ways. (p. 123)

This is another indication of the base of assumption from which people operate with regard to competition and conflict. Most of the resources for which people compete need not be limited. They are limited because of an *assumption* that they are limited. The behavioral patterns that emerge are consistent with this assumption and are reinforced in the context of organizations so that assumptions are met, and one finds oneself in the midst of a self-fulfilling prophecy.

Steele (1975), in *Consulting for Organizational Change,* comments that "competition is simply one instance of a whole class of issues caused by inappropriate transfer of external style to internal organizational processes" (p. 46).

I do not agree with this analysis at all. An individual who has been socialized in competitive and hierarchical social systems does not shed years of social influence and conditioning when he/she enters the organization, particularly if that organization is consistent with the conditioning process.

Elegant survival depends partially on adaption to the system, not resistance to it (that is, survival in terms of the organization). If consistency is a goal (psychological and perceptual), people will behave in competitive ways upon entering these organizations. This is the predictable behavior pattern of individuals in organizational settings.

Slater (1974) states that if war is not available to stimulate technological growth, "competitive greed seems to be a major spur. Technology, in other words, is an extension of the scarcity-oriented, security-minded, control-oriented side in's nature, expressed vis-a-vis, a world perceived as ...oving, ungiving, and unsatisfying" (p. 14).

Since technology is so closely linked to the "good life" in this country, competition as a behavior pattern has always been closely linked to it. The belief that competition is the only behavior pattern and value system that enables organizations to function is deeply imbedded in culture and will indeed be difficult to change.

But competition is not inevitable in organizational life. It is seen as appropriate largely because of the nature of the structure of contemporary organizations, and also because of the reward systems in terms of power, control, and mobility that accompany these structures. Value systems are also a component of this intertwined process of independent and dependent variables.

Values will be examined in some depth in Chapters 5 and 6 as they would exist in a collaborative organization, and as they currently exist in most contemporary organizations.

Tannenbaum and his associates (1974) have undertaken a study of the impact of hierarchy in various types of organizations in a variety of countries. They state that structure is more important than interpersonal perception, and they acknowledge that hierarchy has an impact, but they never quite clarify the exact nature of that impact. One of the recurring themes that runs through much of the work, particularly in the earlier sections, is that hierarchy is an inevitable part of organizations. The culprit is linked to a division of labor. This breakdown of work into its smallest possible components assumes and plans for some mechanism to which to interlock these diverse specialties. Enter hierarchy!

> The maintenance of any social system requires the continuous and successful performance of a variety of activities. There is no known social system in which every member performs exactly the same pattern of activities . . . The de-

velopment of social differentiation is of central importance to our understanding of social stratification because every axis of the former is at least a potential dimension of the latter. Given that one or more properties of social objects are utilized to distribute them to various groups, there is always the possibility that the features used to distinguish one object from another will become not just distinguishing marks, but marks of distinction. In this event, the objects, and the groups into which they fall, will be both differentiated and differentially valued. Thus social differentiation *may* be transformed into social inequality. (Laumann, Siegel, and Hodge, 1970)

When a hierarchy is present, inequality is also present by definition. Competition emerges as a predominant pattern in order to achieve the perceived limited resources of power, control, and authority.

Forces Pushing for Collaboration

A rather comprehensive review of literature on some of the forces pushing for alternative organizational structures and processes, i.e., collaboration, begins this section.

The school systems in the United States are major perpetuators of the competitive model of functioning. The research literature completed in these settings illustrates some rather startling results. The evidence indicates that most students perceive school as being competitive (Johnson, R.T., Johnson, D.W. and Bryant, 1973; Johnson, D.W., 1973; and Johnson, R.T. 1972); that American children are more competitive than are children from other countries (Madsen and Shapira, 1970; Madsen, 1971; Kagan and Madsen, 1971, 1972; Nelson and Kagan, 1972); that American children become more competitive the longer they are in school or the older they become (Nelson, 1970; Madsen, 1971; Nelson and Kagan, 1972; and Madsen and Connor, 1973); that Anglo-American children are more competitive than are other American children, for instance Mexican-

American and Afro-American children (Madsen and Shapira, 1970; Kagan and Madsen, 1971); that urban children are more competitive than are rural children (Madsen, 1967; Shapiro and Madsen, 1969; Kagan and Madsen, 1971, 1972; Miller and Thomas, 1972; and Nelson and Kagan, 1972); that American children often believe that aid to a person in distress is inappropriate and is disapproved of by others (Staub, 1971); and that competition increases anxiety in students performing a motor-steadiness task (Naught and Newman, 1966).

In an examination of the evidence of students performing tasks in school systems, the data continue to grow, indicating that competition is an overriding process with predictable outcomes. Students in competitively structured situations show more anxiety, are less self-assured, and show more incidence of self-oriented needs; students in cooperatively structured situations are less tense and more task oriented (Haines and McKeachie, 1967). Students who are working in cooperative groups are more secure than students in competitive groups (Deutsch, 1949b).

In addition, adults working in large industrial organizations are more anxious when working in a competitive structure than when working in a cooperative structure (Blau, 1954) while 7-year-olds in competitive environments are more destructive, boastful, and demonstrate depreciatory behavior. In collaborative environments they are more sharing, and exhibit helping behavior and friendly conversation (Stendler, Damrin, and Haines, 1951).

There is a vast body of research that supports the proposition that cooperative goal structures encourage positive interpersonal relationships characterized by mutual liking, positive attitudes toward each other, mutual concern, friendliness, attentiveness, feelings of obligation to other students, and the desire to win the respect of other students.[1]

There is also evidence that even when individuals dislike each other intensely or come from groups engaged in high levels of conflict, cooperation in achieving several mutually desired goals produces positive intergroup and interpersonal relationships (Sherif, et al., 1961; Blake and Mouton, 1961; and Johnson, D.W. and Lewicki, 1969).

Further analysis leads to results indicating that low achievers, who pull the performance of the group down, are not disliked or alienated from their peers in cooperative situations (DeVries, Edwards, and Wells, 1974).

Also, under cooperative goal structures, communication among students will be open, effective, and accurate, whereas in competitive situations communication will be closed, ineffective, and inaccurate (Deutsch, 1949b, 1962; French, 1951; Grossack, 1954; Deutsch and Krauss, 1962; Krauss and Deutsch, 1966; Crombag, 1966; Fay, 1970; Johnson, D.W., 1971, 1973; and Bonoma, Tedeschi, and Helm, 1974).

Competition biases a person's perceptions and comprehension of viewpoints and positions of other individuals (Blake and Mouton, 1961) while trust is built through cooperative interaction and destroyed through competitive interaction (Deutsch, 1958, 1960, 1962).

There will be more coordination of efforts, subdivision of activity, and division of labor within cooperatively structured situations than in competitive or individualistic situations (Deutsch, 1949b, Mintz, 1951; and Thomas, 1957).

---

[1]Anderson, 1939; Deutsch, 1949b; French, 1951; Stendler, Damrin, and Haines, 1951; Blau, 1954; Gottheil, 1955; Phillips and D'Amico, 1956; Wilson and Miller, 1961; Sherif, Harvey, White, Hood and Sherif, 1961; Myers, 1962; Raven and Eachus, 1963; Crombag, 1966; Krauss, 1966; McClintock, and McNeel, 1967; Julian and Perry, 1967; Swingle and Coady, 1967; Haines and McKeachie, 1967; Uejio and Wrightsman, 1967; Cook, 1969, Wheeler, 1972; Ryan and Wheeler, 1973; DeVries and Edwards, 1973, 1974; Scott and Cherrington, 1974; DeVries, Edwards and Wells, 1974; Bryant, Crockenberg, and Wilce, 1974; Weigel, Wiser, and Cook, 1974; and Blanchard, Adelman, and Cook 1974.

In order to engage successfully in problem solving, there must be a period in which diversity of ideas and information are suggested and divergent thinking emphasized. This will more likely happen under a cooperative goal structure (Deutsch, 1949, and DeVries and Edwards, 1974).

Individuals will take greater risks in their thinking and actions in a cooperatively structured situation, (Kogan and Wallach, 1967).

Competition may have limited usefulness in organizations. Competition, rather than collaboration, is best when the task is a simple drill activity or when sheer quantity of work is desired on a mechanical or skill-oriented task requiring little if any help from another person (Triplett, 1897; Chapman and Feder, 1917; Hurlock, 1927; Maller, 1929; Phillips, 1954; Miller and Hamblin, 1963; Clayton, 1964; Julian and Perry, 1967; Clifford, 1971; and Scott and Cherrington, 1974).

On the other hand, when the task is some sort of problem-solving activity, research indicates that a cooperative goal structure results in higher achievement than does a competitive goal structure (Almack, 1930; Husband, 1940; Krugman, 1944; Deutsch, 1949, Shaw, 1958; Jones and Vroom, 1964; O'Connell, 1965; Laughlin and McGlynn, 1967; Gurnee, 1968; DeVries and Mescon, 1974; Okun and Divesta, 1974).

In terms of group functioning, cooperative goal structures are more effective than are competitive goal structures in increasing group productivity (French, 1951; Smith, Madden, and Sobel, 1957; Thomas, 1957; Shaw, 1958; Willis and Joseph, 1959; Hammond and Goldman, 1961; Raven and Eachus, 1963; and Crombag, 1966).

One of the major requirements for cooperative functioning is the ability to take the perspective of other individuals (Asch, 1952; Deutsch, 1949a, 1962; Heider, 1958; Mead, 1934; Nelson and Kagan, 1972; and Johnson, D.W., 1974a, 1974b).

Indeed, there is overwhelming evidence that competitive structures and processes are not appropriate for life in organizations. They have consequences that outweight their benefits. They are not good for individuals and they are not good for the organization. Yet they persist. Why? Because of the nature of socialization processes and because of the nature of the major component of organizational life—hierarchy.

In the words of Douglas McGregor:

> External control and the threat of punishment are not the only means of bringing about effort toward organizational objectives. Man will exercise self-direction and self-control in the service of objectives to which he is committed. (1960)

Even before McGregor, organizations were finding ways to thwart the natural leanings of individuals toward working collectively to accomplish goals to which they had developed some commitment and investment.

> We trained hard, but it seemed every time we were beginning to form up into teams we would be reorganized. I was to learn later in life that we tend to meet any new situation by reorganizing; and a wonderful method it can be for creating the illusion of progress while producing confusion, efficiency, and demoralization. (Petronius Arbiter, ca. 60 A.D.)

A dilemma is emerging, one which is related to the structural components of an organization. Leavitt (1972) clearly points out that "structure seems to affect people's feelings in one direction and their speed and accuracy in the other. No one has yet found a structure that maximizes speed and accuracy and, at the same time, morale and flexibility" (p. 194).

This dilemma leads further toward the collaborative model of organizational functioning. Much of the literature in the behavioral sciences has indicated that coordinative approaches are critical when functions, tasks, and/or people are to work together or relate in an *interdependent* fashion. In other words, if the completion of one task or function hinges upon how well another task or function is performed, collaborative structures and processes would be appropriate.

WORK FLOW

> One important dimension of structure that organization charts almost never show is the nature of work flows; because work usually flows over a set of channels different from the authority set. Work, that is, is apt to flow horizontally, without regard for the number of stripes on the shoulders of the people it touches. Very often, in fact, one of the problems of organizational design is the problem of somehow making authority and communication structure consonant with work flow. (Leavitt, 1972, p. 306)

Leavitt's point about making authority and communication consistent with work flow is a critical one. The difficulty is increased because the structure is seldom changed drastically as that would result in tampering with the authority mechanisms already in place and for which people have already adopted rather elaborate coping mechanisms in order to survive elegantly.

Further, since the people whose authority would be changed, and most likely reduced, are usually those deciding whether or not to reduce their own authority; and since people who have power are seldom willing to give it up, particularly if they have had to make some sacrifices and compromises in order to get it in the first place, there is seldom a structure that emerges containing less authority and control for the persons proposing it.

Usually an additional authority-supporting process or mechanism is developed and implemented. This results in another layer in the hierarchy, which the work must "flow" around.

The collaborative model of organizational functioning uses as one of its basic determining components the nature of the task itself. The basic nature of the task is looked at in terms of its interdependence with other tasks, or in other words, the work flow. A collaborative model starts with the nature of the task and builds structures and processes around it, rather than starting with the hierarchical structure and force-fitting the task to it.

ORGANIZATIONAL SIZE

Organizations continue to grow at a fast pace. There are a variety of implications of increasing organizational size. Some of these are:

1. As organizations grow in size, ideas that were useful at one time are no longer useful and a complete redesign is required;
2. A person's organizational fate is determined by people who are at an increasing distance from him/her;
3. Direct communication with decision-makers all but disappears;
4. Increasing size separates people at the same level in the organization from one another;
5. Increased size increases the complexity of communication; and thus:

> increases the probability of misinformation as well as the probability of decreased total information flow. As the number of people between a decision-maker and his [her] source of information increases, the probability of error and misinformation increases — a phenomenon that is most important because of its multiplying effects on attitudes as well as on the quality of business decisions. (Leavitt, 1972, p. 301)

With the increasing size and complexity of many systems and organizations in this society today, and the interdependence of many tasks, it is appropriate to consider alternative organizational structures and processes to those that contain hierarchy, competition, and power attainment at their core.

One perspective, which states that increasing interpersonal competition will increase organizational productivity if certain conditions are met, includes the following conditions:

1. Jobs of competitors are independent, not interdependent.
2. Objective, not subjective, standards for advancement are available.
3. Success for one person can be separated from failure for others.

If these conditions are met, there should be a net increase in productivity in the organization as a result of interpersonal competition (Leavitt, 1972).

The only difficulty with these conditions is that they are almost *never* met; given the nature of today's organizations in terms of increasing complexity, an increase in the dependency on a complex technology, and the increasing complexity of the tasks themselves.

The nature of most tasks (jobs) is that they are interdependent. At the very least there is a strong degree of interdependence between the task and a surrounding technology. Very seldom is a situation found where one person is able to accomplish his/her task without some active involvement on the part of other individuals. Even if one person can complete a task, or make a decision, or propose an alternative, the process of implementation involves others. The others, then, also must have some understanding or investment in the nature of the task.

As Vroom and Yetton (1973) have implied in their

Decision-Making Model, deciding is easy. Implementation causes the bind, when the involvement of others is necessary to implement a decision in an organizational context. Involvement of others is also needed after most tasks are completed as the tasks are usually done "for" someone else. They have to approve the work, since they usually have some control over the future of the "other" in the organization.

There are not many clear standards for performance in any organization. Success is often defined after the impact of the job or product is assessed. Performance, is what seems appropriate at the time, but the effect of that performance can often only be judged in an historical context. It is compared against how others react to it; how consistent it is with the nature of the authority and control hierarchy; how much change is needed in the current pattern of things; the reputation of people and their departments in the larger organizational environment; and some comparison with market conditions.

Seldom are there clear, consistent standards for advancement, because that would depend on who else is in the "pipeline" and how much room is available. Performance and advancement standards are always compared to the organization in which they exist. And since that organization has hierarchical and competitive structures and processes in the main, behavior, and values as expressed in that behavior, are compared against this larger environment.

Thus, the very conditions that Leavitt and others use to justify increasing interpersonal competition speak even more strongly for a reduction in competition since these conditions are not present in today's organizations.

Another incentive toward alternative organizational structures and processes is a growing split between the hourly worker (or the nonexempt worker) and the manager (or the exempt worker) (Leavitt, 1972). Taylorism, the epitome of scientific management, and its opposite, participative management, have each contributed to this split.

Taylorism, with its focus on the separation of planning

from doing, and participative management, with its focus on the interaction of planning and implementation, have inadvertently contributed to a "clogging" of the boundaries between the two groups. Scientific management is often seen as useful for the hourly worker and participative management is seen as good for management. Together the two lead to stress in the system because they are almost mutually exclusive in the context of contemporary organizations.

This confusion is further compounded in that neither of these perspectives is really consistent with the nature of a hierarchical structure. Scientific management is more closely related, but it is inconsistent with the evolving role of a manager as an integrating agent of the organization.

PARTICIPATION

A collaborative organization would have participation as a core component in its nature. Although this sounds rather simple, there are a variety of conditions that must be met before there is any chance of implementation, let alone success in the confines of an organization. Some of these conditions are:

—agreement that learning from experience is an important issue, and in fact valid;
—the possibility of experimental and tentative solutions;
—agreed upon reciprocity in shared authority and responsibility;
—a *real* (and rewarded) capacity for authenticity among the persons involved;
—patience for the development and movement through false consensus; and

—the ability to agree on what will constitute legitimate data to indicate success or failure of a given decision. (Glidewell, 1970)

INTERORGANIZATIONAL RELATIONSHIPS

Before continuing to focus primarily on organizational relationships, it will be useful to review a body of literature that further supports the thrust for collaborative functioning within organizations — one that deals with the interactions between organizations, or interorganizational relationships. Certainly the environment surrounding the organization influences how that organization functions and how it defines the boundaries and parameters of its capabilities.

Several theorists (Thompson and McEwen, 1958; Levine and White, 1961; Evan, 1965; Guetzkow, 1966; Aiken and Hage, 1968; and Warren, Rogers, Evers, 1975) have been summarized by Schermerhorn (1974) when he says that there is a set of motivations for organizations that involve themselves in interorganizational cooperative activities. He also indicated that there is a strong set of potential costs, which must be borne by participating organizations.

Schermerhorn labels this process "Interorganizational Cooperative Relations (ICR)." *Interdependency* is the major attribute of the process, which also includes *mutual risk-taking* and *joint decision-making*. Interorganizational relations involve limits on unilateral decisions by all parties as indicated by Thompson and McEwen (1958).

There appear to be four sets of variables that are associated as correlates of ICR; (1) organizational goals; (2) boundary issues; (3) normative conditions; and (4) opportunity factors. These variables identified by Schermerhorn (1973) also have an impact on interorganizational relationships, on individuals, groups, and processes within the organization. These impacts will be examined in more detail, as they relate to collaborative structures and processes, in Chapters 6 and 7.

ANTICIPATORY DEMOCRACY

Alvin Toffler has presented some of the issues with which this society will have to deal. He has coined the term "anticipatory democracy" to describe the nature of the cultural and political environment necessary for future survival. According to Toffler (1975), society suffers from two problems: a lack of future-consciousness, and a situation where people are involved in their society, in a way that is "ritualistic rather than real consultation." He goes on to say that:

> Technocratic planning, like bureaucracy, is designed for undifferentiated or simple industrial societies and for slow-change conditions. But the U.S. is no longer a traditional industrial society, let alone a simple one. Hence we need a radically different approach to planning. (p. 229)

Alternatives to planning within the culture and alternatives to planning within organizational structures are needed. The development of mechanisms and components designed to interact with each other and be mutually supportive on individual, group, organizational, and societal levels are also necessary.

> If a man is denied both responsibility and power long enough he will lose the ability to respond to the challenge of the first and to grasp the opportunity of the second. One has only to look at what happens to the youth of the ghetto if they fail to find a job over a number of years. The time comes when they become incapable of performing inside that complex framework of disciplines that make up the average working

situation. So too with society; denied responsibility and power long enough, they show a similar tendency and can become almost incapable of response to opportunity because there is not the habit of self reliance. (Manley, 1974, p. 21)

UPWARD COMMUNICATION

Much of the research done on hierarchical organizations provides support for alternative organizational structures and processes. Read (1962) has provided some additional data to support this contention. He found that upward communication depends on the subordinate's ambition, the subordinate's perception of the superior's power, and the trust between the subordinate and the superior. Communication is restricted when the subordinate sees the superior as having a great deal of power, when there is not trust between the superior and the subordinate, and when the subordinate is highly ambitious.

It seems that these conditions are seldom present in a hierarchical organization. The hierarchical organization leads to ambition, power centered upward, and low trust because of the last two factors. One learns that ambition is the name of the game in organizational life; that power-gaining results in being seen as an individual who is "capable of handling the rigors of organizational life."

Several years ago, Warren Bennis (1964) identified the global issue to which this writing is addressed:

The pyramidal structure of bureaucracy, where power was concentrated at the top — perhaps by one person or a group who had the knowledge and resources to control the entire enterprise — seemed perfect to "run a railroad." And undoubtedly for the routinized tasks of the Nineteenth and early Twentieth Centuries, bureaucracy was and is an eminently suitable social arrangement. (p. 203)

Indeed, evidence is strong that alternatives to the notion that organizations are bound to be hierarchical in nature must be devised. That the outcome of hierarchy is bound to technology is a common assumption. Some would assert that we are bound to hierarchical structures and processes on the basis of technology. And yet, one of the most powerful technologies — management information systems with computer technology — offers a powerful set of reasons why this may not be so at all. The notion that information is power has already been examined. A variety of theorists have focused on this relationship (Pfeffer, 1978; Tuggle, 1978). Galbraith (1973) bases his perspective on organizational design partially on this process, as does Weick (1969) when he describes organizations as information processing entities responding to organizational uncertainty.

Since information is power, when organizations consider the use of computer technology, and begin to develop structures and processes to utilize this technology in their particular interests, the current power structure is threatened. Individuals and departments fight for control of this data base, since "facts" are often used in the presumption of rationality in decision making and power struggles in organizations. However, it need not be done in this fashion.

> One of the greatest benefits of computer automation, . . . has been the development of group decision making as a staff function rather than hierarchical decision making through line relationships. The unifying relationship in these varying groups assembled for decision making usually is either a consolidated record file (i.e., personnel and payroll functions joined procedurally through a common master record but separate organizationally) or a series of separate record files that are joined together procedurally in a continuous computer operation with input and output cutting across existing organizational lines.
>
> The trend toward group decision making has evolved largely on a voluntary basis. . . . What probably began as a "getting together" for the purpose of coordination and com-

. munication has subtly evolved into something more like "consensus decision making." Generally, however, the person upon whom the responsibility for a decision would be expected to fall, from an organizational standpoint, would be considered by the group as having acutally made the final decision. This, again, points up the increasingly complex line-and-staff relationships now involved in decision making in highly computer-oriented organizations. (Whisler, 1970)

It is fairly easy to see that technology itself is not inherently designed so that hierarchical organization is the only structure that allows a match between these two variables.

UNCERTAINTY

One of the clearest reasons for the consideration of alternative organizational structures is the uncertainty and turbulence in the environment. A great deal of data has been accumulated to support the notion that an organization needs to be organized in a way that is consistent with the diversity and uncertainty associated with the task being performed (Burns and Stalker, 1961; Hall, 1962; Woodward, 1965; Chandler, 1966; Lawrence and Lorsch, 1967; Fouraker and Stopford, 1968; Hage and Aiken, 1969; Duncan, 1972). It is clear that these data support the need for alternative structures to hierarchy to enter the mainstream of thinking about organizations.

The environment continues to become more turbulent. Raw materials and other resources necessary for an organization to continue to transform inputs into outputs cause uncertainty in terms of availability and appropriateness. Individuals, too, are becoming more aware of their own desires and goals in terms of what they wish to receive from an organization. There is an increasing unwillingness to pay the costs of individual identity, which comes solely from the organization or profession in which one is involved. In fact, more and more individuals are seeking less and less power in the context of organizations. Power is becoming less valid for its own sake as the costs to individuals are realized. One is not "real" in that type of environment; instead, the self is determined on the basis of who is he/she better than, or above whom has he/she risen in the process of climbing the organizational ladder.

It is no longer appropriate for a society, or for members of organizations, or, for that matter, for organizations themselves to act as if "certainty" is very much of a possibility.

Rather, it is beneficial to begin to experiment with and develop those organizational structures and processes that reinforce collaboration instead of competition, and further those that reinforce people as individuals to develop the high degree of tolerance for ambiguity that will necessarily accompany these structures and processes.

Warren Bennis (1966b) has already made a similar prediction. Bennis has described three major thrusts in the American way of life. These are: choice and freedom, collaboration, and science. In Bennis's view, these three are intertwined and lead him to describe collaboration as:

> the most ancient necessity, and it must surely preempt Darwin's emphasis on "competition." The price of competition, seen in Herman Kahn's "Doomsday Machine" and "Dr. Strangelove," is costly; we are committed to living together. (p. 2)

People are committed to living in organizations and social systems. It seems vital, then, to look seriously at the mechanisms that are needed for this new adventure in social reality. The time has come to strive for organizations that are consistent with who its members are, without sacrificing all that they can be.

The current organizational structure helps to develop only what one already is. There is no stretching, no facilitation of people as individuals. They are part of a larger system, which is in existence because they continue to be-have in the same ways.

Organizations do not behave; individuals do! And yet, the profound influences that social systems have on behavior patterns, as well as on value systems, cannot be under-estimated. Both are exposed and acted upon.

Bennis has given this message before, and as yet it has not been acted upon:

> I see democracy, collaboration, and science as three broad streams moving steadily toward a confluence in the twentieth century. (1966b, p. 2)

Bennis's prediction should be applied to the twenty-first century, for it may take that long to learn the vocabulary and fully develop the vision of collaboration. The vision and the belief that it is ultimately possible and necessary must precede the journey for the nation, the society, and, for that matter, the world.

Chapter 5

VALUES IN A COLLABORATIVE ORGANIZATION: AN INDIVIDUAL PERSPECTIVE

One of the clearest aspects of the focus on values in a collaborative organization revolves around the fact that they must be independent variables in our life and functioning in that organization. They must be considered when social systems are reorganized, and they must be considered when appropriate new structures and processes are determined. The impact of socialization on the value system surrounding competition and the reinforcement of that socialization in organizations has already been examined. Human beings have developed reasonable mechanisms for rationalization to insure consistency between values and behavior. They also see the social systems as created by and for them, rather than recognizing that, while this may have been true originally, it is no longer so.

Organizations are now created to perpetuate themselves; their existence becomes the primary goal, and people's existence in them is secondary to organizational survival.

If this process is to be changed, a new value base must be developed. This value base will not necessarily lead to new behavior patterns or new social systems; rather, devoting attention to it will enable people in organizations to discern more accurately the behaviors that are likely to accompany it. At the same time they will get a better idea of what the nature of the context and the reward system will be, in order to optimize support for these new behavior patterns.

Collaborative organizations have a very strong value base imbedded in their foundation. This in itself does not distinguish them from contemporary organizations, which also have a strong value base.

The differences emerge in the conceptualization of alternative organizational structures and processes. First, values would assume more of an explicit posture. That is, they would be recognized as critical in the functioning of a social system, and would be acknowledged as a given in organizational life. Second, the value system would be seen as an independent variable in the concepts and applications regarding organizations. Values would be seen as influencing structures and processes, rather than becoming a mere by-product of organizational life.

This chapter focuses on making explicit some of these values, including openness, trust, concern for others, honesty, power sharing, power expansion rather than equalization, and collaboration rather than competition. Conflict is not positioned as necessarily healthy, or even an integral part of organizations.

Thayer (1973) clearly states the scope of the problem:

> Only the removal of competition will enable individuals in organizations to discover how humanely they can behave toward one another. The logic of competition is one of fear, of being driven out of business, of losing out on promotions, of being fired, of losing status. This dictates the military model of organizations, and the resultant combination of

hierarchy and competition only accelerates alienation. (p. 134)

There is a perspective on organizational life that suggests:

> Organizations are ideas held in the human mind, sets of beliefs—not always compatible—that people hold about the ways they should relate to one another. Within these relationships, people act to realize values, to attain goals important to them. (Greenfield, 1973, p. 560)

Individuals have a whole set of expectations about what is expected of them in the organization. They also possess a set of values that impact on their lives and behaviors in that organization. These values have been learned through the socialization processes imposed by families, school systems, and organizations. The organizations perpetuate the values, and reward the behaviors that are consistent with organizational expectations, and organizations hold considerably more expectations than individuals possess.

In order to break this pattern, organizations must consider changes in structures, processes, roles, rewards, and technology, so that new values can be determined. Individuals are already moving toward the adoption of new values in places outside formal organizations, and this movement has an impact on the types of expectations they bring to today's organizations. The process is likely to continue, and may create severe conflicts and difficulties for organizations of the future unless they now begin to rethink their involvement in the lives of individuals. Organizations should strive to possess and reinforce values consistent with those developing among individuals, by replacing competitive values with collaborative values wherever possible.

TOLERANCE FOR AMBIGUITY

One of the values that is clearly part of an organization's functioning in a collaborative fashion is its tolerance of ambiguity. Filley and House (1969) indicate that an important responsibility of a manager in the current organizational environment is to develop and implement mechanisms and processes for the reduction of ambiguity.

Emphasis on reduction of ambiguity facilitates dependence on the status quo for the purpose of prediction and security. It does nothing to help subordinates (or superiors, for that matter) develop skills to foster and prosper in a higher state of ambiguity. When planning is placed solely in the hands of the manager, ambiguity is reduced on the part of those who are not involved in the planning process, and the probability is increased that their investment and involvement will not be very high.

The development of tolerance for ambiguity as a statement of value in and of itself has a negative connotation in that it is to be "tolerated."

In a collaborative organization, ambiguity itself would become a valued commodity. The development of ambiguity as a solid value base would lead to individuals being able to develop a greater sense of readiness, which could lead to a higher skill level and a greater degree of commitment to the tasks and goals of the organization.

A VALUE INDEX

Slater (1970) postulates the necessity for a *human value index*. He indicates that this is a criterion that assesses the ultimate worth of an invention or a system in terms of its total impact on human life; i.e., in terms of ends rather than means. Slater does not go into detail about what components would be constructed, and how, but the point is still a valid one in that social systems would be assessed in terms of values (this is closer to the assessment of the process) rather than in terms of effectiveness of output attainment.

Perhaps this ideal is utopian. Yet an examination of the literature and of life and functioning in organizations has shown that the idea of a human value index may be a necessity in the not-too-distant future.

UTOPIANISM

Before becoming too involved in studying organizations based on contingency models, let us question the assumptions upon which actions of our organizations have been based, particularly some perspectives on so-called ideal or utopian systems.

> Past efforts to build utopian communities failed, because they were founded on scarcity assumptions. But, scarcity is now shown to be an unnecessary condition, and the distractions that it generates can now be avoided. We need not raise the youth of our new utopia to feel that life's primary gratifications are in such short supply. Hence the only obstacle to utopia is the persistence of the competitive motivational patterns that past scarcity assumptions have spawned. Nothing stands in our way except our insidious dreams of personal glory. Our horror of group cohesion reflects our reluctance to relinquish these dreams, although they have brought us nothing but misery, discontent, hatred, and chaos. If we can overcome this horror, however, and mute this vanity, we may again be able to take up our original utopian task. (Slater, 1970, p. 150)

Philip Slater, in this same text, *The Pursuit of Loneliness: American Culture at the Breaking Point,* indicates that the cultural framework in this country is changing. An apparent change in the value system is underway, resulting in the placement of different values on certain processes and outcomes, as is apparent in comparison of Slater's perception of the old culture with his perception of the new culture (Slater, 1970):

Old Culture		New Culture
Property rights	over	Personal rights
Technical requirements	over	Human rights
Competition	over	Cooperation
Violence	over	Sexuality
Concentration	over	Distribution
Producer	over	Consumer
Means	over	Ends
Secrecy	over	Openness
Social forms	over	Personal expression
Striving	over	Gratification

> The core of the old culture is scarcity. Everything in it rests upon the assumption that the world does not contain the wherewithall to satisfy the needs of its human inhabitants. From this it follows that people must compete with one another for those scarce resources, lie, swindle, steal, and kill if necessary. (Slater, 1970, p. 103)

There may be a scarcity of some natural resources needed to sustain life on this planet, although conservation and the development of alternative resources and patterns of resource use could solve this problem. The abundance of materials that might be available for food in the world's oceans has barely been touched.

However, physiological resources are not the subject of this work. The subject of this work is psychological resources, or resources based on perception. They are equally important. In fact, one might argue that they are even more important to the quality of life than physical survival alone.

Much of the scarcity to which humans respond in organizational life is self-made.

> A pervasive value in the organizational milieu is competition. Competition is based on the assumption that desirable resources are limited in quantity and that individuals or groups can be effectively motivated through competing against one another for the possession of these resources. . . . Collaboration, on the other hand, is based on the assumption that the desirable limited resources can be shared among the participants in a mutually satisfactory manner and, even more important, that it is possible to increase the quantity of the resources themselves. (Thompson and Davis, 1969, p. 79)

This perception of scarcity is a critical factor in the current reliance on competition as the preferred behavior pattern in organizations. Indeed it is not necessary to give up valuing influence over one's own destiny, or even recognition of efforts and skills in the organization. Instead, organizational efforts must be refocused so that goals are more readily attainable by everyone in the organization, and not at the expense of others.

According to Argyris (1975), his Model-1 variables govern individual actions in organizations. These variables include:

1. Achievement of purposes, from individual perspectives alone;
2. Maximization of winning and minimization of losing;
3. Minimal eliciting of negative feelings; and
4. Rationalizing and minimizing emotion.

These are the processes that are already used in organizations. But a higher value must be assigned to different processes and perspectives in the collaborative organization. Model-2 strategies for interaction are most appropriate if organizations are to function differently. Not only must there be a change in the organizational processes, but there must also be a change in the degree to which individuals value these new processes. They must become important as *values* to both individuals and organizations.

> The behavioral strategies of Model-2 involve sharing power with anyone who has competence and who is relevant in deciding or implementing the action. The definition of the task, the control over the environment, is now shared with all the relevant actors. Saving one's own or another's face is resisted because it is seen as a defensive nonlearning activity. If face-saving action must be taken, then it is planned jointly with the people involved.
>
> Individuals in the Model-2 world seek to find the most competent people for the decision to be made. They seek to build viable decision-making networks in which the major function of the group is to maximize the contributions of each member so that when a synthesis is developed the widest possible exploration of the issue has occurred. (Argyris, 1971, p. 482)

Again, the point is made that individuals must come to value these processes as important in and of themselves. Only then can a move toward designing organizations and organizational processes supporting the value base be undertaken.

Some authors have advanced a specific theory for collaborative and postindustrial organizations. Carew (1976) indicates that the values necessary for a collaborative organization are: (1) individual fulfillment; (2) social equality; and (3) ecological balance. Trist (1976), with his focus on postindustrial society, postulates some values that must be present within individuals' and organizational systems: (1) self-actualization, (2) self-expression, (3) interdependence, and (4) capacity for joy.

Neither of these authors has identified totally new value systems; many of them have been discussed in the literature of management and behavioraal science for several years. The authors' major premise is, again, that these values must be more a part of the organization itself. The values must be seen as *enabling variables* rather than just by-products of the process.

Trist's focus on the new values in postindustrial society, so-called collaborative organizational structures and processes, can best be understood as a natural development from current organizational functioning. It is not something that has only recently emerged; rather it is the next step in an evolutionary perspective on the human condition and the mechanisms necessary in social systems to be consistent with them.

Collaborative organizations result from a new gestalt, emerging out of some new permutation of the old and the new. "Postindustrial values represent retrievals, rediscoveries of preindustrial values which have diminished, or lost, in industrial society" (Trist, 1976, p. 1014). Quite simply, individuals are moving from achievement toward self-actualization; from self-control toward self-expression; from independence toward interdependence; and from endurance of distress (grin and bear it) toward a capacity for joy (Trist, 1976).

THE NEW VALUES

The new values, which must characterize a collaborative organization, should be viewed from two perspectives. This chapter examines those values more closely tied to individuals, while the next chapter discusses values that are more closely tied to organizations.

This is, in some ways, a false dichotomy, in that there must be an interdependence and a reciprocity between the two sets of values. They must be mutually reinforcing if they are to flourish and have any impact on individual as well as organizational behavior.

> New values will become salient only if experience in all parts of the lifespace consistently supports their emergence. Therefore, what is happening in organizations has particular importance in that it will effect the character of the task environments in which the individual is likely to find himself [herself]. (Trist, 1976, p. 1019)

While organizations clearly need to support these new values, individuals also need to consider them congruent with other parts of their lifespace, their internal perspectives, and their involvement in other social systems, as well.

Trist (1976) identifies three types of social patterns, and Morris (1956) has made some helpful distinctions regarding value systems. From a combination of their frameworks emerges the values necessary for a collaborative organization.

Trist's three domains are:

1. Cultural values carried by members of the social aggregate;
2. Organizational philosophies embodied in the practices of the formal organizations to which he [she] belongs in various task environments; and
3. strategies of 'social ecology' through which governments and interest groups (at any level) seek to regulate the contextual environments of society. (p. 1013)

Morris's distinctions include the following:

1. Operative values—preference of one object or objective rather than another shown in the behavior of individuals;
2. Conceived values—individual preference for a symbolized object, i.e., cooperation is the best approach; and
3. Objective values—an objective preference, even if it is not conceived of as desirable.

For purposes of this work these can be categorized thus:

1. *Conceived cultural values*—those values primarily carried by individuals; and
2. *Operative organizational philosophies*—values held by the organization and made operational in its structures and processes.

CONCEIVED CULTURAL VALUES
(VALUES OF INDIVIDUALS)

Conceived cultural values are values held by individuals. They are values that regulate behavior patterns, and they are critical for the individuals' survival and continuation of the species. In other words, they are the values that influence everyday behavior, and are important for long-range growth and development: trust, openness, honesty, and growth; self-actualization; capacity for joy and effective functioning; responsibility and dependability; cooperation; and energy, synergy, and homonomy.

Trust, Openness, Honesty, and Growth

These values are interdependent, each being necessary for the others to be effective.

Trust implies a basic belief about one's own goodness and the goodness of others. Trust contains an understanding of one's own motives and the motives of significant others, as well as potentially significant others. It involves a readiness to experience new forms of interaction with others as well as with one's self. It has as a core the ability to anticipate and minimize risk, but not to avoid risk as a potentially growthful process—one that helps individuals to understand their own boundaries of selfhood and the boundaries of others as a condition for understanding one's self.

Trust requires an ability and a willingness to examine one's self in a critical fashion, while remaining open to life as an ever increasing and expanding set of experiences. It embraces growth as a certainty, while recognizing that growth takes many forms and contains many stages that are not always known at the beginning. It revolves around the desire to "plunge into" something without really knowing what the end product will be or where the "plunge" will eventually lead. It is "being open to experience" with an equal emphasis on both the "open" and the "experience."

Trust is more than a mere appearance of realism; it is a continual effort to make that realness become a reality in relationships with others. A trusting person is in touch with the wholeness of his/her being and is able to communicate this to another on an ongoing basis.

This cluster of values may sound a bit "Eastern" in explanation. It is quite a different perspective than that most of us use in terms of behavior and value systems in organizations. Yet it seems that it is not too far removed from the fantasy many have of organizations. Relaxing after work and talking in a frustrated and angry way about bosses and colleagues who did *not* value these things today at work is commonplace. At best, they did not exhibit behavior patterns that infer they held these values in high esteem. Perhaps this is the key. They did not behave in ways that led to the belief that they valued trust, openness, honesty, or growth.

Ultimately, people's behaviors tell others what their values are. "I'll watch what he/she does, and then I'll decide if I believe what he/she says." Or, "that person is two-faced, he/she says one thing, and does something else. I don't trust him/her."

If collaborative organizations are to work, they must be consistent with a value base. They must be what individuals value in their "social system life." So, while those things valued by individuals are the starting point, it must be kept in mind that both are necessary so that there is no inconsistency between the individual and the organizational systems.

Self-actualization

This term probably appears in every reference to individuals striving to be more human and organizations trying to be more humanistic. It is Maslow's term, but even he was uncertain what it really meant, or whether it was an ideal for a tiny number or reachable for the masses.

Self-actualization is a necessary condition for an individual's psychological survival. It is pursued all the time in the form of higher strivings to make the most of what one can in a given situation. It is an attempt to beat the odds when knowing that there will always be odds. Discerning what it takes to survive elegantly in the organization and trying to accrue all those things needed to survive are part of the self-actualization process. It is maximizing what one can get, what one can do, and who one can be, given the boundaries (restraints) of a particular environment.

Everyone engages in some form of self-actualization— and if they're still there, they are fairly adept at it. The problem with this perspective is that, in organizations, most have to do whatever they're doing at *someone else's expense*. That is the nature of a competitive, hierarchical organization. It is consistent with a perceived scarce resource pool, which is reinforced and facilitated by the structure (vertical differentiation) of organizations.

The suggestion here is not to change all basic values, just some of them. A self-actualization process that occurs at someone else's expense, or one that takes place on someone else's terms, must cease. The process has to be on the "actualizing" individual's terms, and it must be done in a way that doesn't impinge on the freedom of others to actualize in a similar manner. It also means being excited about who one is, what one is, and what one can still become.

> One cannot have good feelings for others unless one has a fund of good feelings in oneself. This means being on better terms with oneself than most people are—being less alienated from one's real self by a false self. (Trist, 1976, p. 1016)

In line with this perspective, self-actualization involves the individual's knowledge of who he/she is and what he/she can become. These thoughts are at once different and yet intertwined with each other, forming a larger gestalt. Accepting this duality is the process that enables individuals to become all that they can; at the same time, it enables them to accept and be excited about what they are, who they are, and what they value.

Capacity for Joy and Affective Functioning

These values are also linked, in that both are necessary in order for either to be present. The capacity for joy and affective functioning involves the ability and the continuous desire to experience pure delight! It is that temporary absence of control that accompanies the fervor when we are so happy that we cannot stand it a moment longer. It's the excitement of accomplishment and the feeling of attainment of an "impossible" goal or objective. It's also being in touch with one's feelings; knowing what the feelings are; and being able and willing to express those feelings at the moment they occur. It's having a wide range of feelings that encompass a wide range of behavior patterns without getting locked into a cause and effect relationship.

The ability to experience pleasure, a love of life that is pervasive throughout all behavior, is critical. It is not always a positive feeling in a specific situation, but there is always some degree of satisfaction when the feeling is experienced at all.

This individual joy is linked to the willingness and the expectation that others will be striving to do the same in their own individual lifestyles. One's own joy must not be predicated solely upon an internal focus, but must also be tied to the same experiences on the part of others in the lifespace. Because there is an interaction and an interdependence between the joy of the self and the joy of others in a particular social context, another gestalt emerges.

Pleasure alone, or the mere expression of caring and love, is not enough. "So far as this 'pleasure principal' prevails, joy cannot become linked to interdependence and allow homonomy to balance autonomy in a new value configuration" (Trist, 1976, p. 1017).

> The experience of positive affects is founded on the recognition and experience of interdependence. These give the conditions for the person's realizing his [her] independence; as he [she] can only become whole (can only undo his own psychological splitting) by recognition of the contribution of the other. (Trist, 1976, p. 1018)

Interdependence is critical upon examination of individual values, just as it is critical when the focus becomes the organization. In fact, interdependence is another critical value for individuals.

Responsibility and Dependability

These values are also interdependent. They involve a commitment to the other as a part of the self. They involve a focus on consistency between the internal and the external as well as a caring for the other. They mean that "I-can-count-on-you-and-you-can-count-on-me," but that does *not* mean "I-am-responsible-for-you," nor "you-for-me." Individuals are responsible for themselves, but are committed to each other. This enables them to be themselves. This consistency is dependable. It does not mean predictable in an absolute sense, but rather a striving toward consistency. It connotes goal-directed behavior, while at the same time realizing that goals are not static.

Cooperation

Cooperation is a value that is extremely consistent with a collaborative organization. It involves a muting of boundaries so that they are better meshed as a part of a larger endeavor. Cooperation is not so drastic as compromise, but it does involve some small degree of "smoothing the rough edges." It strives toward establishing interlocking objectives and realizing that this is a *process*—thus, by definition, ongoing and continually changing.

Energy, Synergy, and Homonomy

Individuals in a collaborative organization must value the generation of energy and those situations in which energy is both generated and dissipated. This is, of course, a psychic energy that is generated by open-endedness and synergistic expectations in the situation.

Synergy involves seeking the next level of interaction, the next level of analysis, or the next steps in the process. It rests on the notion that something "greater" can always emerge out of a process or an interaction. It is a gestalt, which assumes that the emergence of a new phenomenon is expected and that the emergence is valued in and of itself. The outcome then becomes a source for the continuation of the process.

Homonomy is a belief in the collective or the larger community. In this context, it is a collective of individuals, where the individual is still the major unit of analysis, but with awareness that the individual exists in a larger system, which interacts with and limits his/her existence in the system. Homonomy recognizes that the boundaries of the individual and the system are indeed permeable and intertwined. In fact, the boundaries of one system help determine the boundaries of the other system. Neither can be very clearly defined without reference to the other. The definition of one helps to define the other. Each system places constraints on the other, and fosters possibilities that would not be attainable without considering the relationships and interdependencies of both systems.

These values are rather revolutionary and far reaching in character and scope. Yet, they are consistent with the core of human existence. One of the underlying themes of this work has been that the role of organizations must become more consistent with who people are. If people are to change organizations, then they must be willing to look at who they are and who they wish to become.

This is a frightening responsibility at times. The fear

can be reduced if one realizes that he/she is not free unless he/she recognizes those controlling forces. Certainly organizations control individuals therein. But individuals also sacrifice control to the extent that they do not realize the things they truly value. They, in fact, give up control to social systems.

The current values acted upon by individuals were given to them in the form of reward systems and structures in organizations. This situation will not disappear, but, as a precondition for change, individuals must acquire different values. They will continue to be at the mercy of the social systems unless they do so.

"We have come to the end of, we are satiated with, the 'objective' valueless philosophies that have always worked to preserve a status quo, however archaic" (Oates, 1972, p. 53).

> The death throes of the old values are everywhere around us, but they are not the same thing as the death throes of particular human beings. We can transform ourselves, overleap ourselves beyond even our most flamboyant estimations. A conversion is always imminent; one cannot revert back to a lower level of consciousness. (Oates, 1972, p. 54)

Chapter 6

VALUES IN A COLLABORATIVE ORGANIZATION: AN ORGANIZATIONAL PERSPECTIVE

This chapter continues the discussion of values in a collaborative organization from the perspective of the organization. The organization will be the unit of analysis as opposed to the individual who was studied in previous chapters.

OPERATIVE ORGANIZATIONAL PHILOSOPHIES

Operative organizational philosophies are those values held by the organization, and operating in organizational structures and processes. What those values are and why they are important in collaborative organizations will now be examined.

Organizations do not really hold values as entities in and of themselves. Rather, the values involved in the organization as the unit of analysis are those embedded in the organization's structures, processes, interactions, and interdependent functions. Individuals in organizations implement the processes and structures, but the processes and structures must have an explicit value base if they are to be consistent with collaborative organizations. This explicit value base will now be addressed.

Operative organizational values include:

—Pluralism, the collective, and a community gestalt
—Power generation
—Functionalism
—Problem finding and problem solving
—Participation
—Consensus
—Support systems
—Nurturance
—Energy creation
—Theory Y assumptions
—Cooperation and cooperative creativity
—Feedback
—Autonomy, individual differences, and respect for differences
—Homonomy
—Freedom and equality
—Expansionism, growth, and nonalienating jobs
—Freedom of expression
—Unbounded consistency
—Interdependence

Pluralism, the Collective, and a Community Gestalt

One of the most critical and complex values is pluralism. Pluralism involves an interdependence between differing individual values and a recognition of interdependence between the individual and the collective. It is synergistic in that it assumes that more is created because of the interaction of different perspectives than merely the camouflaging of differences. It assumes that the whole is greater than the sum of its parts (a gestalt perspective), but it takes into consideration that without both individual perspectives and the perspective and consideration of the collective, something is missing. It is a perspective that says the whole cannot be considered without considering the individual parts. It also says that the individual parts cannot be considered without considering the importance of the relationship of the parts to the greater whole.

Pluralism involves the notion that both sets of variables—the individual and the collective (organization)—must be understood and responded to in terms of their dependency and influence on the other. Individuals need not lose their identity in the organization, but organizations are more complicated than merely a collection of individuals who always have to be considered as the only operating entity.

Pluralism is an inclusive value rather than an exclusive variable. It recognizes complexity and simplicity but does not assume that these are opposite ends of a continuum. Pluralism is a core operative organizational philosophy in our concept of a collaborative organization.

As Trist (1976) hypothesizes:

> The capacity to accept the greater degree of pluralism that is characterizing the transition to postindustrialism and which involves loss of paramountcy in any one value or "figural" societal system will be a function of the extent to which a unifying ground can be established. (p. 1024)

This unifying ground is one in which the collaborative models are operating. It allows for thinking in a unified perspective as well as in ways that facilitate an examination of the component parts of the processes.

Power Generation

Organizations must value the generation of power rather than its containment or reduction. Power, or its less value-laden partner, influence, must be seen as useful—in fact necessary—in the functioning of the organization. Current organizational functioning assumes that power must be limited and that there is not and should not be enough to go around.

Collaborative organizations would value the establishment of functions and tasks where individuals could demonstrate their ability to influence, without using that influence at another's expense. Influence is an expectation that would be met; it would be assumed that individuals are capable of having and using influence and that they would function in ways that would increase the opportunities for influence on the part of others.

Power and influence would increase at a geometric rate rather than remain as a static process. Current organizations value power shifting rather than power generation, which results in a slight decrease in the amount of power available. A self-fulfilling prophecy contrary to the other that currently exists in organizations would be established. If people expected that they could approach situations in ways that generated more influence for others as well as for themselves, the amount of influence "available" in tasks, processes, and structures would surely increase.

Functionalism

Functionalism implies a movement in the direction of focus on function rather than on role. It also involves a movement away from function as a vertical differentiation. For example, the behavior pattern of coordination is often associated with a "higher order" function than some task specialty such as sales or underwriting. It is often assumed that coordination or supervision is "more important" or more difficult or more complex than other functions in the organization. It is often associated with the role of supervisor or manager. Yet there is no inherent need for this to be so. The hierarchy of roles in the structure places some higher in the hierarchy than others. This leads to the perception and behavior pattern that reinforces this placement. These begin to appear *more* important rather than *as* important functions, along with a variety of other functions within the organization.

Organizations must value a functional focus, which excludes a major emphasis on a vertical distinction for its continuation. Rather, the function must be valued for its own sake. It must be compared with other functions that are necessary for task completion. Generally, there are a variety of functions that need to be performed for the successful completion of the task. If any of these are not completed, the task is not completed. It is not that coordination is any more important than a particular specialty.

Organizations must place a value on this functionalism rather than on vertical differentiation as a major discriminator of important roles in the organization.

Problem Finding and Problem Solving

Organizations must value both problem finding and problem solving as linked processes that are mutually interdependent for organizational functioning. Ingalls (1976) has described these two processes at some length.

Problem finding involves the discovery of a situation that might need some responsive action taken. It involves a diagnostic capability seldom rewarded in current organizational contexts.

Organizations often reward problem covering rather

than problem finding. It is imperative that problems not surface that would make the superior look ineffectual, or worse yet, incompetent. The only rationale for uncovering problems is if a solution is already available, preferably one that makes the proposer look good. This leads to the likely prospect that the "problem" will be thought of primarily in terms of solution rather than cause. It fosters solutions that make symptoms disappear, but not the underlying causal variables. Those underlying variables often dictate a challenge to the existing authority hierarchy, and thus are rarely confronted directly or exposed as they exist.

Problem finding requires some large degree of creativity if potential problems are to be explored in any depth. Creativity is not likely to emerge if trust is low, or if people are worried about their careers in terms of mobility. Ideas are often judged as "good" or "bad" on the basis of who is presenting the idea. This does not facilitate the building process, which is necessary if fear and resistance are to be kept separate from the expectations of power and control.

Individuals must feel free to examine situations in terms of multiple causation from interpersonal dynamics through social system considerations to structural or technological considerations. Without this freedom, only narrow perspectives, consistent with the broad organizational norms and expected problems that emerged in previous problem finding processes, will be reinforced.

Problem finding also involves a heavy affective component as a part of the process. People must be expected to become "emotional" as they elucidate positions and attempt to find out what is just beneath the surface. Emotions in and of themselves are not "bad." They are an integral part of organizational life. The negative potential of emotions arises when they are used *exclusively* as a stimulus and rationale for supporting a particular position or problem statement.

Problem finding also encompasses the ability to tolerate ambiguity. It means that one expects, in fact welcomes, situations that are not clear-cut or simple. One also welcomes an examination of those situations that do not have neat, tidy, prepackaged solutions. People are often very impatient in organizational settings to "get on with the solution" since that is the "real" work of the organization—or so the managers keep saying.

Some degree of ambiguity must be accepted in the notion that separates the problem finding process from the problem solving process.

Problem solving is a more rational process than problem finding. This is natural since most of the work has been completed in the problem finding process. Solutions should "flow naturally" out of the definition and statements of the nature of the problem. Problem solving involves implementation.

The most critical component of any action strategy is determining who will do it, and how it will be done. Many problems, accurately diagnosed, are never "solved," because the solutions are never implemented. Hierarchy and competition do little to generate investment in outcomes that really deal with problems. They are much more oriented to perpetuation of the status quo.

If done in a collaborative and participative fashion, problem finding generates investment; problem solving identifies a particular specified solution that is to be applied to an already "identified" problem. The problem finding process has already generated a great deal of investment and agreement on the nature of the problem. The problem solving component, then, is the implementation of a tentative solution with an evaluation of that solution built into the process.

The problem finding/problem solving process is not totally rational, since only one problem and one solution are identified. If it were that easy there would be no need for the process at all. The problem and the solution would be self-evident.

The important value statement here is the linking of the two processes, as well as the recognition of the importance of the problem finding component of the larger linked process. This is a clear example of the embedded nature of values in organizations that strive to function collaboratively. The structures and processes contain these values within them in such a way that an almost indistinguishable interaction between the value and the process results.

Participation

Participation is a very broad value that would have to exist in a collaborative context. While it is hard to argue against in the abstract — especially in a democratic society —participation is seldom considered in organizational life. Individuals rarely are involved in decisions that affect them or in decisions in which they may be able to contribute valuable insights.

The need for greater participation has increased in importance in postindustrial society as organizations have become more interdependent. A great number of decisions are being made within organizations affecting a great number of individuals and subsystems within the organizations, which speaks very strongly for the need to develop more participative structures and processes. Again, values must play a more pivotal role in organizations of the future, and participation certainly emerges as one of those pivotal values.

Participation results in a higher degree of investment and a higher degree of commitment to the final outcome. It results in greater feelings of importance by individuals for the entire social system as it is exemplified in one particular decision-making process. In contrast, from one or two nonparticipative situations, individuals tend to develop a general pattern of noncaring or noninvolvement, which is consistent with most larger organizational structures.

Thus, participation for its own sake is justifiable, at least as a way for people to change their expectations about the major variables at work in a particular organizational setting. Of course, this value would have to be embedded within the framework of the organization. Decisions regarding involvement or noninvolvement of specified individuals or departments would have to be made with this consideration firmly in mind.

It would be better to have too much participation than too little. Indeed, it is difficult to conceive the possibility of too much participation.

> If one could abandon the idea that only one person must be responsible for organizational decisions, it might be possible to put more honesty and realism into executive decision-making. The lonely vulnerability of the executive could be reduced quite a lot. It seems to me that the relief might free him [her] from trying to be something he [she] can never be, whether he [she] tries to be the unflinchingly rough and tough competitor, the unrealistically wise and knowing mentor, or the unbelievably slick and cynical sophisticate. The dependency of his [her] subordinates on his [her] objectivity could be considerably relieved, and the relief might free them to express their ideas and feelings more openly. The executive's search for hard data on *the*, not *his* [*her*] decisions in action could be significantly extended, and they might free the whole system to depend upon concrete data rather than upon abstract authority for the resources they need in the search for organizational competence. (Glidewell, 1970, pp. 95-96)

Consensus

Consensus is not a new idea or a new value. It is, however, often misused by advocates of humanistic decision-making processes. It does not mean that everyone agrees on a particular outcome. It does mean that everyone has been involved in the process, and that everyone agrees to test a particular outcome for its workability.

Most decision-making situations do not have as an inherent component only *one best* solution. If such were the case, there would be no need to *decide* anything. Consensus involves the complete exploration of a particular situation with the recognition that there are going to be conflicting points of view, and that it is important that these come into the open during the process. These differences are not resolved just because a decision is reached.

Individuals who are not in agreement with the "majority" perspective do not just give up their differences and comply with the majority. They sit back and wait for some way to sabotage the outcome, or to say, "I told you that wouldn't work." These outcomes are likely because a competitive process is established where the goal is to "win" rather than to arrive at a "workable" outcome. Since winning is the predominant goal, all of the dynamics described earlier emerge in a miniature form during this process.

Stereotypes of both parties influence what they hear the other party saying, and power gaining, rather than power generation is the outcome. A nonconsensus decision-making process results in the dominant coalition in the process or larger organizational context retaining their power base, and the lesser coalition looking for ways to regain their perceived loss of influence. Immediately they begin to develop strategies to regain their lost "clout" and prestige, or at least to minimize their overall loses by gaining ground in other parts of the organization or in future decision-making situations.

Consensus is a critical value for organizations, not because it is good in and of itself (although that is true), but rather because it leads to better quality decisions, with more investment in implementation. There is less focus on decision making to protect organizational boundaries and authority distribution, and more focus on decision making to solve difficulties facing the organization.

Support Systems

As an operative organizational philosophy, collaborative organizations must adopt support systems that are built into the formal organizational structure. It may not be necessary to develop separate systems for this purpose, since the values already identified have an implicit support component built into them. Participation, consensus, functionalism and pluralism have support as a by-product of their effective functioning.

In the short run, specific mechanisms must be in place to support individuals and departments as they move toward a collaborative system. Even if an organization is functioning in a collaborative fashion, there will be a need for specific individuals or groups who are identified as places for support in the ongoing functioning of the organization. This is so because there will still be differences of opinion and different perspectives on how to function in a specific situation.

Support systems are also necessary to help individuals learn about some of the dysfunctional aspects of their behavior. Defense mechanisms are necessary for handling the conflicting stimuli that occur daily in complicated environments. These conflicts will not go away; rather organizational mechanisms must be devised that will help individuals develop an awareness of how these may be obstructing more effective interaction in the organizational context.

One of the mechanisms by which people attempt to gain favor in some circles is the mentoring system. A mentor is someone in the organization at a higher level who teaches the "ropes to know and the ropes to skip." It is that individual who helps figure out the maze of organizational hierarchy and the centers of power and influence. Mentors accept some responsibility for movement in the organization.

In a collaborative organization, there would be no need for a mentoring system in the same way that it is now utilized. It would not be necessary for an individual to shepherd another through the hierarchy of authority since that would not exist in its current form. The mentor then becomes someone who is a primary center for support in sorting out interpersonal issues that may be affecting an individual in the organization, especially those that impact task completion in the context of the organization.

Mentors would not function as therapists; they would not be exploring deep-seated or long-standing personality issues with the individual. Rather, the mentor (a function, really) would be helping individuals sort out the issues important to them, identifying those areas in which they possess strengths of use and importance to the organization, and helping with a prioritizing process, which would lead to action, in behavioral terms, for the individual and for the organization.

Nurturance

Nurturance involves a concern for the individual as a whole person, a concern for the perspectives that are important for him/her, and an emphasis on continued development of feelings, attitudes, and values. It is a developmental value in that it is always forward looking, always concerned with potential rather than static, current skill orientation. Nurturance is based on the premise that individuals have almost unlimited potential to respond to change and complexity in an organizational context. In order for this potential to be realized, support must be given for the feelings held by individuals in the organization.

Nurturance has a connotation of caring. It is *not* a neurotic caring; it is a nurturant caring where one is concerned about another for his/her own sake. It is an explicit recognition of individual differences without building an entire organizational framework on this premise.

Collaboration is based on the realization that individuals are more similar than they are different, that social systems have had the predominant socializing effect in the development of behavior patterns, and that value systems are an integral part qf this socializing process.

Given these variables, the development of the particular differences between people fosters individual growth, and links people together *via* a process of nurturing that overrides the existing individual differences. The ultimate objective becomes providing and fostering processes that are supportive of individuals even though there are differences between them.

Energy Creation

The need for organizations to foster power generation rather than power gaining has already been discussed. It is also important for organizations to value the creation of more energy from individuals, rather than to focus on energy depletion.

John Ingalls (1976) has written a book entitled *Human Energy: The Critical Factor for Individuals and Organizations* in which he discusses the need for creation of energy, or excitement, as a basis for behavior, commitment and investment in the life and functioning of the organization. He speaks of the need to develop alternatives to a hierarchical model as a source of energy development. Organizations must adopt the creation of energy as an operative organizational philosophy, and come to value individuals with a strong sense of excitement rather than adaptation, and investment rather than co-optation.

Energy creation assumes that individuals have a great deal to give to organizations, but unless excitement and commitment are highly prized by the organization, it is unlikely that individual energy creation will happen — in fact it probably won't happen.

Theory Y Assumptions

It has been 20 years since McGregor (1960) first identified the Theory Y assumptions that characterize organizations. And yet, organizations are still basically structured as if they held Theory X assumptions about individuals.

Theory Y assumptions must be valued by the organization in terms of their operative organizational philosophies. Assumptions and expectations influence behavior, and if organizational structures and processes lead to individuals' perceptions that they are seen as incapable, lazy, and needing to be controlled (Theory X), they will soon act in ways consistent with these assumptions. Thus, a change in organizational structures and processes is necessary to bring about some consistency between organizational structures and processes and Theory Y assumptions.

Cooperation and Cooperative Creativity

The outcomes of cooperative functioning and competitive functioning have already been compared (Chapters 2 and 3, primarily). An implicit commitment on the part of organizations to cooperation, in terms of the Constitution and a democratic value base, is necessary. It has not, however, found its way into organizations, nor, really, into the culture itself. Instead, competition, compromise, and adaptation are firmly entrenched. People "cooperate" in ways that maintain their own power base and keep others from gaining more power. They also "cooperate" to perpetuate the pervading hierarchy of authority, to exclude others from a piece of the action in terms of mobility and advancement. They have yet to learn the value of cooperation in terms of interdependence, synergy, support, nurturance, or creativity. Until this type of cooperation is valued to the extent that competition now is, and holds as revered a position in operative organizational philosophy as competition now does, there will be no significant changes made toward developing cooperative creativity. Not until the current value orientation changes can the situations described by Studs Terkel in the introduction to *Working* change.

> This book being about work is by its very nature about violence — to the spirit as well as to the body — It is about ulcers as well as about accidents — It is above all, about daily humiliations — To survive the day, is triumph enough for the walking wounded — for a Monday through Friday sort of dying.

Cooperative creativity has been mentioned previously in the discussion of problem finding. Creativity is seldom evident unless the "old" ways of doing things are cast aside so that people can visualize a new way of doing things.

The ability to get outside of the situation must be developed to enable individuals to "see" what is going on "inside" of the situation. Because they often get "locked" into their current perspective, help and nudging from others is often needed so that they can determine the "forest from the trees." This is a building process, where one builds on ideas from another; where the community or cooperative gestalt facilitates coming up with a better product or idea or plan than any one person is able to do alone.

Cooperative creativity is an implicit component of several of the previous operative organizational philosophies, yet it is important enough by itself to deserve mention as a necessity in a collaborative organization.

Cooperation is somewhat synonomous with noncompetition, as it is used in this context. One of the difficulties with the examination of alternatives to current structures and processes is the vocabulary used to describe organizations that in theory are democratic, but in fact differ vastly from democracy in its ideal state.

Cooperation is often used to imply a compromise or a negotiation. That is not the use intended here. Here, it means a mutual sharing of resources and control in a way that neither party is denied an outcome because of the other party, nor does either party achieve an outcome because of the outcome of another party.

Feedback

Feedback, as used here, refers to both the interaction of the organization with its larger environment, and the interaction of individuals and groups with each other and the social system (organization) within which they are embedded.

Trist (1976) has a rather poignant comment about the former:

> To succeed in a problem-continuing environment, postindustrial politics must become both more participative than the politics of industrialism, more developed and more open to rapid and continuous feedback. Postindustrial man [woman] will spend more of his [her] time in politics than industrial man and more in the planning processes associated with it. In all likelihood, he [she] will have the leisure time to spend in such activities. (p. 1028)

Organizations will need to value ways in which the data about the organization and its interaction with its environment are shared with individuals in the organization. Organizations must value processes that clarify what the processes actually are, what impact they have on individuals, and how this data impacts the organization's products.

This is an information-sharing perspective that is consistent with a collaborative organization and with the other values that have been previously examined, especially power generation. Since information is power in an organization, this information must be widely shared in the organization's functioning. Many who have this information will not be willing to share it because of fear, or some statement like "they won't know what to do with it," or "we can't let this out just yet." If organizations value feedback rather than "feed nothing," the statements by Trist would make no sense.

Perhaps the most critical aspects of feedback are those concerned with individuals and groups and their interrelationships with the larger organization. Feedback is essential in knowing how one is doing in the organization. Even if it is not received directly, it is easy to look around in the organization to find some mechanism of process to interpret as personal feedback. People need to know how they affect the system, and to a somewhat lesser degree, how that system affects them.

In order to move toward tolerance of ambiguity, people need to know what is going on around them in terms of their impact on it and the individuals who are a part of it. They need to know others' expectations, and they need a mechanism to communicate their expectations to others. This information is *not* to increase certainty, but to enable them to evaluate their options as they assess the impact of various behavior patterns on themselves, others, processes, and outcomes.

This feedback serves not to pinpoint an exact position,

but rather to serve as reference points in an ongoing movement in the context of the organization.

Much of the human relations literature stresses that feedback should be nonevaluative. That may not be possible. Feedback might be more accurately called *responsivity*, as it is really more of a reciprocative responsiveness between individuals and the organization. A person needs to know how he/she is doing, and shouldn't be punished for that responsivity; however, there will be some evaluation in most responses received and given in the organization, and in interpersonal feedback as well.

Autonomy, Individual Differences, and Respect for Differences

Implementing a value system consistent with a collaborative organization may, on the surface, appear to have some inconsistencies. One of the characteristics of a collaborative model is that it strives to develop mechanisms that are primarily interdependent in nature. It strives to rise above unidimensional models of issues impacting on human behavior in an organizational context. It is a type of contingency model wherein everything is related to everything else. It is a systems model in that action in one part of the system impacts on action in another part of the system. Autonomy raises all of these issues.

Autonomy facilitates the development and functioning of each unit of analysis (individual, group, or collection of groups) as if it were a unique entity, at the same time recognizing that it gains its identity partially from the system in which it is embedded.

Autonomy involves creating permeable boundaries, while recognizing that boundaries are necessary for definition of the entity in question. It conveys the freedom to develop in an organic and evolutionary fashion without getting trapped by predetermined outcomes from the entity or from the boundaries. Autonomy recognizes the uniqueness of each entity while viewing the similarities as the connecting or linking points to other entities. It is freedom with perspective, rather than freedom with restraint.

This is indeed a complicated philosophy to apply; yet it is necessary to start with this as a value in order to move toward application.

Autonomy also involves a recognition of individual differences and a respect for those differences. The synergistic interaction of those differences results in cooperative creativity, synergy, energy creation, power generation, and a community gestalt. Even in discussion of the operative organizational philosophies necessary as independent variables for ogranizational functioning, one cannot be discussed comprehensively without some reference to the others. They are interdependent, but they must be viewed and understood partially on their own merits and characteristics. They must also be considered in terms of their interaction, impact, and consistency on and with the other values previously postulated.

Homonomy

Homonomy refers to the collective or the community. It is that system surrounding the individual. It is the collection of individuals making up an organization, and the collection of groups making up a social system. It is counterpoint to autonomy, implying that boundaries influence what is within the boundaries. One might say it puts limits on autonomy, however, it is preferable to think of it as a facilitator of autonomy, and as a mechanism that facilitates movement past autonomy in a synergistic movement toward interdependence of individuals and the collective.

> We are now able to recognize that our minds belong, quite naturally, to a collective "mind," a mind in which we share everything that is mental, most obviously language itself, and that the old boundary of the skin is no boundary at all but a membrane connecting the inner and outer experiences of existence. (Oates, 1972, p. 53.)

Oates gets a bit philosophical, yet she is on to the essence of homonomy. Part of homonomy recognizes an inevitable interdependence of individuals in a worldwide setting—a recognition of "sameness" over "differentness." She has framed the issue in terms of individuals, but it could just as easily be framed in terms of organizations.

From one perspective, organizations must recognize that individuals are the organization. This really means that individuals are a *necessary* condition for the organization to survive. They are, however, *not* both necessary *and* sufficient for the continued survival of the organization. Organizations need structures, processes, a technology, and some task focus. If taken alone, none of these are sufficient conditions for the continuing survival of the organization. Organizations must apply philosophies that are consistent with the premise that the "collective," with all of its interdependent subparts, influences and is influenced by all components of the collective.

Freedom and Equality

Both freedom and equality must be valued in a collaborative organization. Freedom allows the individual to do his/her own thing in a context that supports this variety, with little concern for the impact of a particular act on someone else, or with little regard for the impact of the act on some outcome or reaction of the act.

Equality, on the other hand, focuses on the *impact* of a particular act on someone else, or on the outcome of a behavior or attitude. It is the boundary around the individual; it is the restraint on total spontaneous behavior and thought. It implies that all have the same freedoms as long as they do not infringe on someone else's freedoms.

The interaction between freedom and equality is similar to the interaction between autonomy and homonomy. Each interacts with the other, and neither can be understood or implemented without reference to the other. In organizations, individuals interact with structures and processes, and the reverse is also true. Collaborative organizations would value the interdependence between these two variables. The tension and dynamic equilibrium that emerges must be valued as important in and of itself. Suppressing these tensions into a hierarchy of authority and a competitive process defeats the move toward a collaborative organization. Predictability and a reduction in these tensions is the present objective. Collaborative organizations must strive for the reverse of this. Recognizing the importance of this tension in the creation of synergy and energy, as well as investment and excitement for the life of the organization is extremely important.

Expansion, Growth, and Nonalienating Jobs

Most jobs and tasks are designed for and perceived by the occupants to be reductionist in nature. Organizations break tasks down into their smallest possible components, and individuals are expected to conform to these job design parameters. Neither the nature of the task itself nor the individual is expected to be reinforced for expansion or growth, in terms of job responsibilities. "Do your job," is the commonly heard response to requests for nonalienating work. "Your job is important, we need you," is a response that ignores individual desires to grow, develop, and operate with some degree of flexibility in the organizational context.

Collaborative organizations value the development of

jobs and tasks designed to expand over time, rather than remain in a static state. The current organizational outlook defines promotions as a method of expansion — both for the organization and the individual. The individual has always responded (conformity) to the hierarchy of authority. This has always been the way to "move up" in the organization.

Expansion has always been an upward movement through the hierarchy. To remove hierarchy as a major organizer and separater, organizations must come to adopt a different perspective on expansion for individuals. They must adopt an operative organizational philosophy that focuses much more clearly and specifically on the nature of the tasks performed in the organization. Tasks, rather than hierarchy, must become the crucial factor. Tasks need diversity, creativity, and fluidity built into them. Each task must have within it the capacity for a variety of functions to be performed. These functions may not be hierarchically different from each other, but must all be seen as crucial for successful completion.

Organizations must appreciate growth on the part of individuals; this is consistent with expansion of tasks. This particular type of growth would be both psychological and skill-oriented. Keeping in mind the Theory X versus Theory Y assumptions about the nature of the human species, it is important that organizations recognize the need to go beyond McGregor's theses. Not only must organizations "act" as if they hold Theory Y assumptions about individuals, they must also support behaviors that are likely to emerge with this type of assumption base. They must respect change in individual perspectives, as well as a continued development of in-depth perspectives about organizational functioning and task accomplishment.

Organizations must also support a reward system that reinforces the ambiguity held by individuals.

Individuals must develop an increased tolerance and "expectation set" around the nature of their jobs. This may, from time to time, create some confusion on the part of an individual about what next steps should be taken to complete a particular task; it may also result in some pressure to regulate processes that should remain fluid. There must be some underlying anticipation on the part of the organization that this tension is only a temporary state that leads to an ultimately more synergistic approach to task completion, with a higher quality outcome and a higher level of task completion.

Freedom of Expression

As members of the organization, individuals have few guarantees of freedom of expression.

Ewing (1977) presents a rather dismal picture of the degree to which legal systems support individuals speaking out on issues that are of concern to them. The probability of a premature dismissal lurks everywhere. This certainly has an effect on the likelihood that individuals will be willing to raise issues close to the heart of a particular organization or a particular product.

Ethics have a way of becoming a relative variable in current organizational frameworks. A particular task is completed and then the rationalization that explains and justifies the actions is developed. It is an "end justifies the means" philosophy, which, if carried to extremes, results in control and coercion of the worst kind as each individual or subsystem struggles to justify his/her/its own outcomes.

Individuals have to be supported in their right to express their opinions as they see them. The organization must respect this free expression as vital in its overall functioning. It must value it completely, for to value it partially is not to value it at all. The organization must, in fact, build into its ongoing actions those mechanisms that not only facilitate this openness and free expression, but go so far as to reward individuals who are "up front" with their input on task design and completion, structural development and implementation, reward systems, and any other additional facets of life in the organization that come to their attention.

This candid thrust must be an integral part of the lifestyle of the organization, and not be relegated to smoke-filled rooms or after-hours meetings in private locations. Some of the structures and processes that must be in place to support this operative organizational philosophy will be discussed in later chapters. Suffice it to say that freedom of expression as well as other operative organizational philosophies previously identified must be integral parts of the life of and in the organization.

These philosophies must be viewed and supported as independent variables in a conceptual sense, since they influence other variables or outcomes of the organization. They cannot be merely passing considerations along with a variety of other inputs into the functioning of the organization. They are particularly critical in the changeover from a competitive organization to a collaborative one. After that change has taken place, and individuals have been socialized to a new set of expectations in the organization, values become less important in the perpetuation of collaboration. They don't become unimportant; rather, structures and processes that have been implemented in a way that is consistent with these values emerge as mechanisms that perpetuate the new behavior patterns that complement these values.

The values in and of themselves are not both stimuli and reinforcers, but remain as variables consistent with behaviors that have emerged and are reinforced in collaborative organizations.

Unbounded Consistency

The individual is a system unto himself/herself, existing within a larger system that has boundaries similar to those of the individual. Current organizations are structured so that the boundaries between the individual and the organization are accentuated. One system cannot meet its goals without adversely affecting the other system. This might be labeled bounded inconsistency.

Boundaries between individuals, between departments, and between individuals and departments and the larger organization are rigid. Organizational structures and processes accentuate the solidifying of boundaries at the expense of mechanisms to cut across these boundaries. Subgoals within the organization are rewarded and yet there are no real rewards for increasing the permeability between the boundaries.

Unbounded consistency results in less development of "separateness" and more development of "similarness." Energy is not directed toward maintenance of a territorial mentality, with the preservation of the status quo emerging as the only dominant factor in ongoing organizational life. Unbounded consistency emphasizes overall consistency between operative organizational philosophies, conceived individual values, organizational structures, and organizational processes. Consistency between all of these variables is still considered an operative goal. This is not done by establishing rigid boundaries between different subsystems within the organization. Solid boundaries between departments are not encouraged.

This is also consistent with functionalism, which focuses on function rather than on the organizational unit or subsystem to which one belongs. Since the hierarchy of authority and the resulting competition is not present, there are no additional pressures to fortify boundaries or to amass power at someone else's expense.

Promotions in competitive situations are not a primary process, so there would be less likelihood that individuals who perceived a lack of opportunity from the structure would band together and establish norms contrary to the organization's task accomplishment. Consistency increases, but the need for boundaries is reduced, or one hopes, eliminated.

Interdependence

Much of this chapter revolves around *interdependence*. All the values are related to each other to form the "gestalt value" necessary for a collaborative organization to exist and function. Synergy and power generation, and pluralism and functionalism, and synergy and feedback certainly interact with each other to the mutual benefit of both values.

In fact, most of the values and operative organizational philosophies can be understood and implemented only in terms of their interaction and consistency with other values mentioned.

Interdependence between autonomy and homonomy, and between task and authority are two of the more critical interrelationships that have been examined. This interdependence, if implemented in terms of consistent structures and processes, can result in what Trist (1976) has labeled a "negotiated order." This negotiated order would result in less fragmentation in organizations, in the culture, and in individual interactions. It would require massive rethinking about organizations and culture. This reformulation would "involve substituting for an order based on the competitive challenge of superior power, a *negotiated order* based on mutual accommodation of interests all considered to be legitimate" (p. 1020).

> The idea of a negotiated order is congruent with the need to develop a greater capability to manage interdependence through cooperative rather than competitive relations, (although not without confrontation). (p. 1021)

Collaborative organizations, which will come about

through and as a result of a new "negotiated order," will contain consistent relationships between values, structures, processes, and outcomes. This is a normative perspective, except for the notion that there is still no *one* "ideal" structure or process that is appropriate for all situations.

Further, collaborative organizations are always in a state of some fluidity, in that the process of defining the parameters of a particular project are as important as the project itself. The fluidity of the process also helps with increasing boundary permeability between and among various components of the process.

In current organizations, the value systems are considerably different from the ones necessary for a collaborative organization. Contemporary organizations stress exclusive achievement of the organization's objective, cognitive rationality, and a lack of support for emotions as viable variables in human and organizational interaction. They also facilitate unilateral direction, coercion, and a reward system consistent with these values. Hierarchy and competition are two of the major organizational variables that reinforce this value system.

The contemporary film and record, *Saturday Night Fever,* includes a song that exemplifies the feelings of many in our organizations:

> It's all right, it's okay
> You can look the other way.
> Life goin nowhere, somebody help me
> Life goin nowhere, somebody help me.
> I'm stayin alive
> I'm stayin alive
> Whether you're a brother, or whether you're a mother,
> You're stayin alive.

Recall the scene in the film where John Travolta's father tells him that the raise he (John) got is lousy and too small, and that it doesn't mean anything. John becomes very upset with his father and forcefully tells him that he is a fool and doesn't understand: it's not the raise that matters, it's the fact that somebody paid attention to him.

In an article entitled "Work and Serenity," Ralph Siu uses a parable to describe the ways in which individuals must behave in order to avoid exploitation in an organization.

> Observe the cormorant in the fishing fleet. You know how cormorants are used for fishing. The technique involves a man in a rowboat with about half a dozen or so cormorants, each with a ring around the neck. As the bird spots a fish, it would dive into the water and unerringly come up with it. Because of the ring, the larger fish are not swallowed but held in the throat. The fisherman picks up the bird and squeezes out the fish through the mouth. The bird then dives for another and the cycle repeats itself.
>
> Why is it that of all the different animals, the cormorant has been chosen to slave away day and night catching fish for the fisherman. Were the bird not greedy for fish, or not efficient in catching it, or not readily trained, would society have created an industry to exploit the bird? Would the ingenious device of a ring around its neck, and the simple procedure of squeezing the bird's neck to force it to regurgitate the fish have been devised? Of course not. (p. 5)

Exploitation of individuals comes from greed, talent, and a capacity for learning. These are the ingredients the organization needs to complete its performance. So, it fosters these needs in individuals, and then proceeds to meet them, claiming that this is "the way people are." If you are somewhat greedy, have some talent, and are able to learn, *and,* if you do not wish to become exploited in current organizations, then you have limited choices. You should hide these qualities.

This continued exploitation of individuals is part of what leads to the pursuit herein of the values, structures, and processes of collaboration. Work in our current patterns of organizational life can be characterized as an *escape from freedom.* It offers the opportunity for socialization — in someone else's mold; and for identity — from someone else's perspective. People are often unaware of the degree to which their identity comes from who they are and what they do in organizations. It's what people are told very early in the relationship.

Collaboration offers a *return to freedom* — freedom for both the individual and the organization. Freedom from the traditional constraints of hierarchy and competition. Freedom from always knowing who you are, because of what someone else is or did. Freedom from always having to look over your shoulder, to see if they are after your piece of the power. Freedom from self-definition in the organization's terms alone. Freedom from one-upsmanship in creative endeavors in the organization, and freedom from covering up emotions and being told, "Don't get emotional. Let's be rational about this."

Further freedoms emerge when one can participate in decisions that affect his/her life in the organization, and from not always having to be his/her own support group. Freedom from not knowing what others think and whether they are responding in terms of who someone is, or in terms of what someone can or cannot do to or for them in the organization. Freedom to express joy, and caring, and developing a new energy level in the organization and in life outside the organization. Freedom to be who you are, and what you are, and what you can become. Freedom to be inconsistent at times and consistent at others. Freedom to value the collective and yet to be focused in terms of an individual sphere of influence.

This is where collaboration leads us!

Chapter 7

COLLABORATIVE ORGANIZATIONAL STRUCTURES

This chapter presents the patterned arrangements and relationships that emerge in a planned or semi-planned fashion and surround the life processes of the organization. It is difficult to completely separate the structure of the organization from the processes that accompany this structure. However, those issues specifically related to the formal structural components of the organization, including hierarchy, control, vertical differentiation, reward systems, roles, and conceptual models, will be the focus of this chapter, as will be a variety of examples of collaborative structures in organizations.

The distinction between structure and process is a somewhat artificial one, but process will be included in the discussion as it makes the nature of a particular component of structure more understandable and coherent.

Perhaps an analogy to the human body will further explain the distinction between structure and process. One of the major systems in the human body is the circulatory system. That system is comprised of veins and arteries and the blood that flows through them.

Although it is possible to understand the circulatory system without understanding blood characteristics and functions, the understanding of both these systems is enhanced by an understanding of the component parts. For similar purposes, the structure of an organization (the veins) and the processes of organizations (the blood), as well as the relationships and interdependences of these two variables will be examined. The understanding of each and both together is enhanced by discussing the relationships in this format.[1]

In collaborative organizational structures, one of the primary issues addressed is that of hierarchy and the control processes that emerge in this structural arrangement.

DEVELOPMENT OF HIERARCHY

Marglin (1974) provides some startling insight into the development of hierarchy. His analysis is economic in nature, and he states that the "social function of hierarchical work organization is not technical efficiency, but accumulation" (p. 62). His ideas, developed at great length with a thorough review of historical perspective surrounding the industrial revolution and resultant industrial development can be summarized as follows:

1. The capitalist division of labor *guaranteed* an essential role to the entrepreneur in the production process; as an integrator of separate processes into a marketable product;
2. The success of factories came from gaining control of

---

[1] I am indebted to my colleague Tom Dulz, at the University of Hartford, for this analogy.

the work *process* and the *quantity* of output, and in fostering a change in the choice of how much to work and produce to a choice of whether or not to work at all (this is hardly much of a choice); and

3. The accumulation of capital as a social function of hierarchical control of production.

There is evidence that hierarchy did not emerge because it was necessarily superior to *all* other methods of organizing, but rather as a function of control processes.

This analysis also suggests that collaboration must be proposed and supported with the awareness that organizations have an influence over value systems. It is not enough merely to propose a change in value systems. This will not magically lead to a change in those mechanisms that perpetuate values and behavior patterns. Eiseman (1977) discusses a model for collaborative problem solving that asserts the implicit notion that if individuals simply satisfy the desires of other, collaboration will result. Eiseman states:

> The collaborativeness of a process depends not upon the extent to which all activity is carried out jointly, but rather upon the extent to which it is guided by the commitment to fully satisfy everyone's basic, conflict-relevant desires. (p. 314)

This statement reflects a lack of basic understanding of the impact of social systems, particularly structures, on the behavior of individuals who are part of the system. It assumes that individuals are able to act or will act with little or no regard to the environment or structure that surrounds their behavior. This view is naive, since individuals don't exist in a vacuum; if they did, they might well have given up the dysfunctional behavior of conflict and competition long ago.

Trist (1976) has identified some of the changes in the

nature of organizations that can be expected in the transition to postindustrial society (p. 1019):

Industrial Era	*Postindustrial Era*
Mechanistic forms	Organic forms
Competitive relations	Collaborative forms
Separate objectives	Linked objectives
Own resources regarded as owned absolutely	Own resources regarded as society's

Likert (1961) indicated that the classical organizational structure provides interactions between superior and subordinates as individuals, but makes no provisions for interactions between the superior and the group as a whole. Likert would substitute for this model of a "cooperative motivation system" the model of a group oriented management. He argues that organizations should be run on the basis of mutual influence of members, similar to a pluralistic notion in government. One of the consequences is more effective communication, since the group can communicate ideas to the superior that no one individual would communicate alone. He also states that effective group action should stimulate individual motivation since there is a great deal of opportunity for high-level identification with the group goals when individuals are involved in their formulation.

Beckhard (1969) based his philosophy on organizational development on the need for competing groups to move toward a collaborative way of functioning. He discussed the need to move toward "high collaboration and low competition between interdependent units" (p. 14).

Hierarchy places individuals in a fantastic bind. If an individual is part of the organization, he/she is an instrument of the organization, and this can be responsible only when taking action contrary to the decisions of the organization (hierarchy) (Thayer, 1973). Organizations thus foster mindless individuals who are adept at the party line but who have lost their own individuality along the way. They have lost touch with their own value system, their feelings, and have diminished the boundaries between themselves as entities and the larger organization of which they are a part.

Fisch (1961) indicated that the distinction between line and staff functions in organizations is inappropriate, and argues for the substitution of what he calls a "functional teamwork" form of organization. He indicates, however, that the supervisor handling each type of job would have "appropriate" authority.

The notion that formal organizational authority must accompany supervisory roles doesn't seem to disappear, and probably won't be dispensed with until the need for fewer supervisors is recognized.

Bass (1964) conducted a study where the use of a classical line-staff organization was compared with an organizational structure based on Likert's (1961) concept of overlapping committees (and linking pins). The formal arrangement of overlapping committees resulted in greater production, greater profits and sales, and lower inventory costs than the line-staff organization.

Lawrence and Lorsch (1967) viewed organizations as open systems whose internal characteristics must fit the external demands of the environment. Internal relationships are described as intertwined and influenced by "the nature of the task being performed, the form of relationships, rewards, and control, and by the existing ideas within the organization about how well-accepted members should behave."

While Lawrence and Lorsch are generally accepted as contingency theorists, which would include the possibility of a hierarchical model, their ideas are generally consistent with those of a collaborative organizational structure.

COMPONENTS OF COLLABORATIVE
ORGANIZATIONAL STRUCTURES

Functional Differentiation

Functional differentiation is the first component of col-laborative organizational structure. This entails differences in function but not authority differentiation, i.e., horizontal differentiation rather than vertical differentiation.

In the words of Blau, one would "disallow quantitative differentiation of status but stress qualitative differentiation of persons" (Etzioni, 1961, p. 347). Coordination would remain an important function in collaborative organiza-tions, and individuals would need to have functional re-sponsibility for this area. The difference between methods of accomplishing this in a collaborative organization and a traditional organization is that the function of coordination would not be elevated to a "higher order" function (hierar-chical). Instead it would be seen as necessary and compli-mentary to a variety of other functions performed by indi-viduals in the organization.

Currently, coordination has a higher level of authority attached to it than do other functions. It is assumed that function cannot be implemented without additional organ-izational authority attached to it. In a collaborative organi-zational structure, this assumption is not warranted, and the structure is consistent with this perspective.

Generalism in organizational functions seems to be the key here. That is, more individuals will be capable of im-plementing a greater variety of these functions. Since coor-dination should be the responsibility of everyone in the department, the particular individual with this specified function would not need any special organizational author-ity from the organization. His/her function would be to act as a facilitator in the process, as someone who keeps the process moving if it slows down, but not as someone who has final responsibility over the outcome.

Nonelevated Roles

This component of collaborative organizational structure flows from the previous one. In organizations that operate in a collaborative manner, there should be a general reduction in the elevation or raising of certain roles to a position of greater control, authority, or status in the organization. The organization assumes a "flatter" shape, with more specialization. But it also exhibits more generality across functions, with a greater pool of individuals performing each of the functions.

Again, functions such as coordination, quality control, interfacing, and linking with other departments are clearly spelled out, but are not rewarded as if they were more important in the outcomes and processes of task accomplishment for the unit involved. This characteristic is necessary in order to move away from a hierarchy of control in organizational settings. Functions that have a control component attached to them must not be elevated "above" other functions in the organization. If authority of one function over another is considered critical for the functioning of the organization, it should be used very sparingly. Even then, it should be designed so that the core of the authority function is interdependence of task rather than influence to "get someone to do something."

Nonscarcity Structures: Functional Dispersal

Functional dispersal relates to the need for collaborative organizations to remove the variable of scarcity from the structure.

In a hierarchy the perception is that there is only a certain amount of status and prestige to go around. Power is also seen as limited in a hierarchical structure. The very nature of a nested structure (hierarchy) limits the rewards (reinforcements) as one moves "up" the organization. This concept of scarcity nurtures the kinds of competition that are not beneficial to the individual or to the organization. Collaborative organizations must adopt structures that do not contain scarcity as an integral part of their operating methodology. This means that the concept of "up" in organizations must be eliminated; increased complexity, or in-depth technical skill, or depth or breadth of knowledge must take its place. It is a subtle distinction, yet critical to collaborative functioning.

Differences in the ability and desires of individuals to function effectively in organizational environments will abound. Present functioning has eliminated more than the appropriate opportunity levels for individuals in terms of complex or responsible (involved) tasks in the organization. The limits imposed on individual creativity and energy are not consistent with the needs, desires, and capabilities of the human species.

An organizational structure that is collaborative in its outlook is based on *functional dispersal*. That is, the organization distributes functions to a variety of individuals based on the assumption that there are enough to go around, rather than on the assumption that functions are limited and must be distributed selectively as rewards for effectiveness.

From a collaborative perspective, there are *not* inherent "higher" and "lower" order functions in a hierarchical arrangement of authority. Rather, there is a dispersal of functions throughout the entire organization. This dispersal is based on the notion that there are always more functions than there are individuals to complete them, rather than the reverse.

Just as there is a nonscarcity of functions, there is also a nonscarcity of rewards for increased responsibility, complexity, and technical competency. These additional skills involve understanding of group functioning, understanding of individual dynamics and understanding of the values inherent in a collaborative organization. They also involve an understanding of the interdependence of a variety of departments, as well as the behavior that facilitates the interaction of the organization with the culture and society in which it exists.

Further skills involve knowledge and skills of organizational renewal and maintenance of the collaborative structures and processes. Again, it should be noted that these are not "higher order" functions that require a greater degree of control or influence over other equally important functions, but rather those that need to be carried out for the organization to function effectively. They are, however, skills and knowledge-based competencies, which individuals will probably develop after some history with the organization. As such, they may well be performed by individuals who have a longer length of service, who have a greater tolerance for ambiguity, and are more psychologically and emotionally secure. These individuals will tend to be less defensive and more tolerant of individual differences viewing them as strengths rather than as something to eliminate in the search for certainty and predictability.

Reward for Skill Acquisition and Dispersal

In hierarchical organizations, individuals are rewarded for performance, for making their superiors look good, and for conforming to the global expectations of the organization.

In a collaborative organization, performance is expected (within very broad limits); thus, reward systems favor the acquisition of applicable skills and knowledge. They are also set up to establish mechanisms that promote the dispersal of skills and the creation of functions. Consequently, individuals who facilitate the learning of other individuals, and those who increase their function-complexity are re-warded in the organization. The more individuals keep "working themselves out of a job," the more they are re-warded in the context of a collaborative organization. The only remaining hierarchy might be something similar to a hierarchy of complexity in terms of skills to be mastered or knowledge to be transmitted.

The very real danger here is that the organization begins to attach more importance to these greater degrees of com-plexity, which in turn, could cause a move back toward a hierarchy of control and authority. The organization must value this complexity, because it is necessary to survive elegantly, but not because it is indispensable or more impor-tant than others.

Performance Criteria

Collaborative structure must contain some clear, con-cise, *operational* criteria for effectiveness. The lack of these criteria offers hierarchical organizations an opportunity to prosper.

In the absence of criteria for task completion, the posi-tion in the hierarchy becomes the critical determinant of effectiveness. If someone "above" in the structure says that a subordinate has done a good job, then he/she has, by defini-tion, done a good job. Control and authority are mighty determinants of success and failure . If there is something in it for the boss to have a subordinate succeed, then the chances are he/she will succeed. If that success is not in someone else's interest, then he/she will probably not be considered highly competent.

This question of competence also becomes critical in a system functioning on the assumption of scarcity. In hier-archical structures, there is usually some limit to the number of promotions that can be used as rewards. Thus, even if individuals are performing effectively (hard to determine in the absence of clear performance criteria) there are not enough rewards to go around.

This is compounded by guidelines stating what percentage of individuals can be rated "outstanding" in a given department. Thus, even in the best of hierarchical arrangements, not all of those who perform well are rewarded. And for those who are rewarded, more often than not it is for conformity rather than consistent outstanding performance.

One of the clear results of studies of behavior modification is that rewards must follow closely upon the completion of the desired behavior. In collaborative organizations rewards are given immediately following demonstration of an appropriate behavior, rather than on a fixed interval schedule of reinforcement currently used in most organizations.

In order for the dispensing of rewards not to become a means of control residing in the hands of one individual, or a small group of individuals, there is a need for clear performance criteria and outcome criteria for tasks and functions. The dispersal of rewards becomes just that; a distribution of already earned rewards, not the decision making centered in one function of whether or not a reward was justified. While such decision making must be performed in the organization, it is not inherently of a higher order than other equally important functions.

Worker Ownership

An increase in worker ownership involves an increase in worker control over the work process itself as well as the quantity and quality of output. This increased ownership must be built into the patterned relationships of the organization, as well as into the operative organizational philosophies (from Chapter 6). It also involves an increased share of the profits involved in this ownership.

Because there is an increase in functional differentiation and in functional dispersal, this "spreading" of control and responsibility is a natural outgrowth of these components.

Financial responsibility becomes a concern for a larger and larger number of people in the organization as the organization moves toward more and more collaboration. Gradually, the distinction between worker and owner becomes a minor distinction.

There may remain certain individuals who have financial responsibility as a primary function, but at the risk of repetition, this is still not seen as a "higher order" function. Rather, it is simply another function that must be completed for the organization to continue in a society.

In the financial area, as well as in others, the broad criteria of success and risk are jointly determined and agreed upon by a large number of individuals in the organization. Information on the parameters of these decisions is not perceived as scarce or secret, but it is shared across boundaries in the organization. Individuals in other functions continue to develop appreciation, skills, and knowledge of the importance of these variables.

This is consistent with the earlier notions of generalism and nonelevated roles. It is also necessary for only one individual or for a small group of individuals to be in positions of control over others in the organization. Of course this requires established performance parameters that are developed and agreed upon by the individuals involved.

Organic Structures

The idea of organic organizational structure is not a new one. It has been used by a variety of authors when contrasted with mechanistic structures to define a fluid, adaptable, and flexible organizational structure. It has an inherently large capacity to change as new data is generated about the environment or about the requirements of the particular task at hand. It has been primarily discussed as appropriate when the environment is turbulent, when there is a great deal of uncertainty in the environment surrounding the organization. It has also been touted as appropriate when a great deal of "boundary spanning" between the organization and the systems impacting it most predictably describe life in the organization.

Boundary spanning centers on the interaction between two or more subsystems, because this interaction is so critical to the continued functioning of all the subsytems. There is a great deal of interdependence in these systems; each depends on the others to some extent, for their identity, task definition, and task completion.

These characteristics are consistent with some of the components of collaborative organizations and with some of the individual and organizational values that would have to exist if organizations and social systems are to function in a collaborative manner. It is a logical extension, then, to consider that organic structures would be a part of collaborative organizations.

To discuss the need for organic structures and to describe what these would look like involves somewhat of a contradiction. The *exact* nature of a collaborative structure cannot be precisely determined. If it is organic, it is also emergent to some degree. Different structures and different mechanisms for implementation must be redeveloped as new tasks and goals emerge in the organizational framework. Mechanisms that foster environmental sensing and monitoring must be developed and implemented so that data on the impact of the environment can be readily available to individuals inside the system. There is clearly a whole set of roles that must be established for an organization to survive in a larger social environment where choices outside the direct contol of those affected are made.

If collaboration reaches cultural proportions this problem would be considerably reduced; the analysis must be confined to organizations that still exist in this larger social milieu.

In addition to the boundary spanning components of organic structures there are components related to the internal ongoing nature of the organization, including production, accounting, design, and training. Diverse structural components may be necessary for each of these divisions in the organization, but the central issue still remains. It is *critical* to design structures that are flexible, fluid, and, by *design*, able to adopt as causal conditions change or are modified.

In addition, the notion of *emergent* designs or structures is a critical consideration for organic structures. Structures often emerge from the task at hand if one is observant enough and flexible enough to see them within the task dimensions. The constraints and parameters of the task itself are often the key in establishing appropriate structural modules, which should be used in a particular set of circumstances. If the task has many individual steps involved in it, coordination and integration will be critical in the completion of the task. If the task has links to other departments or other physical locations, integration and boundary spanning will be critical in its completion. Further, if the task requires a great deal of skill or knowledge for completion, these specialties and support for these specialties (skill and knowledge) will become critical.

It is not possible to detail all of the permutations and combinations for a particular organizational structure to accomplish a particular task. What is important at this juncture is to assure that the structures and the components of structures are organic in nature and fluid so that they can be modified from task to task, or as the development of individual skill and confidence increases.

Linked Objectives

The notion of linked objectives has interdependence as an element; as such the major rationale for it has already been elaborated. It is included here as part of the organization's patterned interaction, which has ties to the formalized components of that interaction (structure).

Deutsch (1973) has presented two contrasting ways in which individuals and objectives can be linked together. He discusses *promotive interdependence,* saying it can be used to "characterize all goal linkages in which there is a positive correlation between the attainments of the linked participants" (p. 20). This is a situation where there is a positive correlation between goal linkages, which can go from 0 to +1.0.

Deutsch also discusses the contrary set of circumstances that are "conditions in which participants are so linked together that there is a negative correlation between their goal attainments" (p. 20). This second set of conditions are those that are *contriently interdependent* and are descriptive of the purest forms of competition. The correlation in this set of conditions may range from−1.0 to 0.

To use Deutsch's term, *promotive interdependence* is the set of conditions that ought to exist to be consistent with linked objectives in a collaborative organizational structure. The goals of one task must be linked to the goals of another task, and the success of one department needs to be linked to the success of another department. Tasks need to be designed in such a way that completion demands dependence upon the interaction of another person in order for each of the respective tasks to be completed.

Linked objectives are clearly tied closely to job design. Jobs must be designed so that there is interdependence built into the *nature of the job itself*. At the same time, there must be a balance so that individuals also have autonomy in how they accomplish a particular task. The linked objectives provide the parameters for the task, including the need for interdependence, but the individual involved must also have some latitude in terms of implementation.

The need for clear performance criteria is also related to this issue. Jobs need to be designed with autonomy in mind; they also need to be designed so that they provide feedback to the individual performing them.

This feedback should come from the *job itself* regarding the design of that job. In order to happen with any degree of impact on performance, the criteria for performance must be spelled out. Feedback in and of itself is relative. It only takes on meaning when it is compared with something else or is interpreted or compared with some other component surrounding it, or is a part of that process or task of which the feedback is the focus. Thus, objectives need to be linked. These links need to be tied to performance criteria about which feedback can be generated, so that the progress toward an objective linked to someone else's can be monitored by the individual performing that function to attain that objective.

Integration and Interdependence

Patterned interactions in organizations must have specified functions that encompass a focus on the relationships and links necessary and sufficient for the completion of the task and the survival of the organization.

In contemporary organizations this is theoretically fulfilled by the supervisor or the individual to whom several individuals report. A problem arises when individuals in the role of authority are more concerned about the issue of authority than the integrating function. Subordinates are concerned about looking good, while superiors are concerned with appearing to be in control.

The superior is also someone else's subordinate, so he/she has to look good, also. With everyone running around trying to look good, integration and interdependence tend to disappear. Further, since everyone has to look good, no one can safely raise the issue of the missing functions for fear of looking bad, at which point they contribute to someone else (their boss!) looking bad as well.

Since they are evaluated on how well they play the game, it is not appropriate to stop playing the game or even to indicate they know that a game contrary to the one in which they are supposedly engaged is being played. (And Catch—22 is alive and well).

Interdependence is critical to break this pattern. It must be removed from the authority of evaluation, and it must be separate from power in the traditional sense of superior-subordinate relationship. Although critical to the overall view of the department and its goals, objectives, and mission, it must not be perceived or designed as if it were more important than the other functions in the organization.

It is also important that the function of fostering interdependence be shared among individuals. It is not advisory that it be used to reward good performance. It may be a function that can be performed by an individual who does not have tremendous technical skill or the expertise to provide in-depth information. One must remember that control does not revert to the individual with the technical expertise or the in-depth knowledge. Rather, influence should be seen as necessary for the task to be performed, keeping in mind that a variety of tasks are equally important in the overall success of a department and ultimately in the overall effectiveness and efficiency of the organization.

Functional Influence

Each function, by design, has an equal probability of influencing the outcome. At various stages in the process of task completion, there are various functions that have a higher probability of influencing the process.

For example, at the begining of the process, the planning function is more likely to influence the process than is the evaluation function. However, since these functions are designed with interdependence in mind, no single function gains absolute control over the process to the exclusion of the others. Influence still remains a viable part of the process, but this influencing is associated with function rather than with role.

With influence being coordinated with function, this framework should lead to more influence in the hands of individuals. It increases the mastery of specified tasks and it moves individuals into a position of controlling more of the work process as well as the quantity and quality of output. Although some control is still vested in the function, control vested in the role of "boss" or "superior" is reduced and ultimately vested in the task to be accomplished. One variable is thus removed from the constant consideration of what/how is this position/perspective related to authority and one's future in terms of a career in the organization.

The behaviors of individuals are more likely to be determined by the task and goals at hand rather than by a superstructure of an authority hierarchy imposed on the ongoing tasks and functions in all situations.

The probable result is more freedom of expression and more trust that the responses of others are more closely related to a particular situation than to their own needs to protect their power base, or to look good to someone else.

Increasing Mastery of Task and Process

Another variable of organizational structure to be considered is that of individual mastery of task and process. All of the variables previously examined have mastery as their goal. It is critical that collaborative structural components have this as one of their outcomes. Individuals gain more mastery over tasks and more skill and knowledge of processes when they feel like they have some influence over design and implementation. A building-block process evolves, which ultimately benefits the individual as well as the organization. This is consistent with functional disbursement, and with the examination of reward systems that reinforce the acquisition of new and more complicated skills rather than those that reinforce perpetuation of the status quo. At the same time, it is consistent with the notion of nonelevated roles — in fact, leads to the elimination of roles in the sense that they now exist in organizations. In current organizational functioning, roles are a series of expectations about what is to be done. This aspect may not change. What will change, however, are the elements of authority and competition that influence current perceptions of roles.

Roles are currently viewed as labels that provide guidelines for performance. A psychological contract evolves as a result of this socialization process, with the "contractee" being ritually accepted and expected to initiate others into the rituals and meanings of organizational life. Mastery of "perpetuation" skills, survival skills, mobility skills, and "saying the right thing" skills increases. What is not gained is mastery of those skills with which to perform the task more effectively. This is not to say that there is not some increase in these skills on the part of individuals during the course of their stay in organizations. It is, however, largely a matter of chance that this occurs, rather than as a part of the reinforcement pattern and planned human resource development.

At the very least it is not consistent with competition and hierarchy that one should learn how to do the task in a better fashion. That one learns the art of elegant survival is consistent. Accomplishing the "job" in spite of the organization, its structure, its processes, and its reward systems is usually learned, as is competing with "class" rather than completing a task or project with elegance.

Boundary Permeability

Collaborative organizations will have more permeable boundaries than do contemporary organizations. The differences between departments and functions become less clear as the functional interdependence in the organizational context continues to increase. There will be greater emphasis on the "weness" than on the "theyness." Movement between functions is encouraged — in fact, it will be rewarded — as the increased attention to functional disbursement begins to impact who one is in the organization and on perceptions of who others are. As the competition between individuals and betwen subsystems lessens in the organizational context, the need to separate individuals and departments in order to gain identity and mastery over career mobility and perpetuation of the status quo is reduced. There is less need for individuals to be concerned with and to behave in ways that lead to consolidation of power and resources.

Rather, disbursement will become a more critical process, as this disbursement takes place, the boundaries and differences, which originally existed to highlight differences, will begin to dissipate in an effort to facilitate the discovery of similarities.

Worker Participation in Other Countries

The United States is not the leader in experiments and successes in the area of participation and collaborative organizations. Although this country is beginning to experiment on a serious level with these options, Europe is far ahead in this regard.

West Germany has laws governing codetermination, and a long list of countries with worker councils and worker representation on supervisory boards includes, Austria, Belgium, Denmark, France, Ireland, Italy, the Netherlands, Norway, Sweden, Switzerland, and the United Kingdom (Hammond, 1974). Yugoslavia and Poland can also be added to this list.

There have been a variety of organizations in the United States that have either experimented with collaboration and given up or are still engaged in some rather innovative structural changes in their organizational composition.

Some of these are: Indianapolis Rubber, Donnely Mirrors, the Vermont Asbestos Group, International Group Plans, Inc., the Chicago and Northwestern Railway, Litton Industries, Kimberly-Clark, General Foods, Inc., and the Saga Corporation.

Legislation in the United States has been noticeably lacking in the area of employee ownership, structural and process issues for organizations, and employee rights regarding a voice in the actual work processes and the control over these processes. Once again, several European countries are ahead in this area, with laws requiring the establishment of work councils as well as laws dictating that organizations be concerned about the psychological health of the workers.

At a conference held several years ago, on the teaching of organizational behavior, one of the attendees, who had recently published a book on international management, was asked why Europe was so far ahead of the United States in this area. His reply was particularly poignant, "Well, perhaps it's because we have had several hundred years longer then you have had, to realize the importance of these issues."

Indeed, that is perhaps true. Europe has also had the luxury of developing at a slower rate without the immediate continuing impact of cultural and technological change. In addition, it must also be recognized that a troubled economy provided major impetus for much of the organizational experimentation in some of the European countries.

Both of these factors may have incited impetus for additional experimentation, and careful analysis of data from current experiments, in the area of collaborative organizational structures in this country.

ALTERNATIVE ORGANIZATIONAL CONCEPTUALIZATIONS

To undertake a drastic revision in organizational structures, to move from those that are competitive and hierarchical toward those that are collaborative and participative, we must eliminate the organizational chart existing in contemporary organizations. This means a movement away from the "pyramid," with its inherent hierarchical structure, and toward some other form of abstract representation of organizational structure.

Ingalls (1976) makes some attempts to begin this process when he talks about the circle or ellipse as a possible model, which provides and reinforces more energy production and distribution on the part of individuals in organizations. Ingalls describes this model as one that contains a variety of interlocking circles, with specified mechanisms connecting them to form a whole. This is one way to design an organization consistent with the components of collaboration.

Viewing a collaborative organizational structure in terms of a *functional responsibility chart* is yet another

FUNCTIONAL RESPONSIBILITY CHARTS

Structural Components

	A	B	C	D
A	Individuals A_1-A_n			
B				
C				
D				

Task Components

Figure 7-1.

approach. There would be at least two of these, and they would be similar to Figure 7-1 and Figure 7-2.

Figure 7-1 illustrates the relationship between the task and the structural facets of the organization. The cells represent individuals who will perform certain tasks using a defined structure.

An unlimited number of individuals could be completing a task within a given structural boundary. This allows differentiation of function but does not infer any "higher order" to any of the functions or tasks.

Figure 7-2 illustrates the relationship between process and structure to be used in the design of a truly collaborative organization. A relationship between structural and process components, with each of the cells becoming a task that needs completion, is illustrated. This type of diagramming allows the organization to do some diagnosis to determine the appropriate task relationship that should exist.

Two other variables should be incorporated into a concept of relationships between structure and process. The

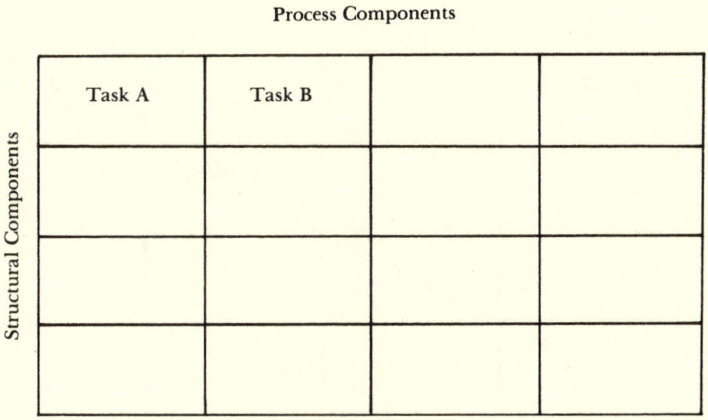

Process Components

	Task A	Task B		

Structural Components

Figure 7-2.

continuum that emerges for *task complexity* (from low to high) can be related to the variable of Task Components. This provides a differentiation between various levels of the Task Components as they relate to complexity. It further allows the formulation of diagnostic decisions that are to be made regarding the degree to which a task is broken down into smaller and smaller parts.

Structural interdependence also requires examination. This variable refers to the degree to which a given structural component is linked to another for it to be able to be operational and have the intended impact. The continuum goes from low to high and shows differentiation between various structural components in terms of their interdependence. As previously discussed, interdependence is a critical characteristic of both values and structure.

Another variable to be considered is the collaborative organization's *reward system*. This is a bit of a diversion from the conceptual models, but it is appropriate to tie the reward system into the relationships between structure, process and task.

There is a great deal written about schedules of rewards and the importance of accurate assessment of behavior, as

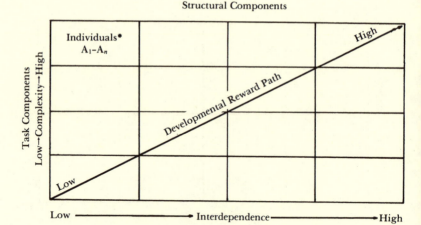

Figure 7-3   Functional Responsibility Chart*

*Cells could also represent departments or departmental clusters.

well as the increasing realization that rewards should closely follow the behavior they reward. Because successful perform- ance and task completion have often lacked clearly defined standards, this has posed a difficult problem for contem- porary organizations. The proposed model somewhat recti- fies that situation.

Tasks and processes can be characterized along a com- plexity continuum while structures are illustrated along an interdependence continuum. *Individuals* are rewarded for the level at which they are able to perform in the organization.

Thus, a *developmental reward path* is established, which moves from low to high depending on the degree of complexity of the task and the interdependence of the struc- tural components within which the individual function emerges. Figure 7-3 illustrates these relationships between

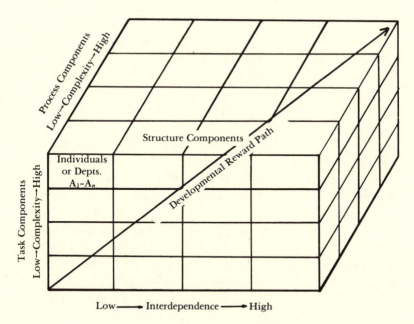

**Figure 7-4   Interactive Functional
Responsibility Chart**

structure, and structural interdependence, and between task components and task complexity.

The entire set of relationships is illustrated in Figure 7-4, which diagrams the three-dimensional rendering of the relationships between task components, structural components, and process components, as well as the relationships between task complexity, process complexity, and structural interdependency.

The developmental reward path is one that moves from tasks with little complexity, simple processes to structural components with little interdependence, to tasks that are complex and require highly complex structures and processes.

Individuals are rewarded for their ability to behave

within the confines of this continuum of conditions. They may also be rewarded for how often they are in particular cells, i.e., with whatever frequency their behavior pattern is in one of the cells at the upper end of the developmental reward path. These cells represent tasks that are generally more difficult, complex, sophisticated and require a greater mastery of a variety of skills.

Returning to the concept of *functional dispersal* brings into focus yet another dimension. Individuals are rewarded for behavior that supports the dispersal of functions throughout the organization and further to the degree to which they were able to help other individuals acquire the requisite skills to implement a greater variety of complex and interdependent functions. The outcome is a reward system that requires clear performance goals and clear reinforcement patterns, and that is tied to complexity of task and process and is interdependent with the structural components. It allows a variety of behavioral responses to the choices made by individuals involved.

There is an inherent danger in this model, one very clearly related to the possibility that individuals performing in the model's upper right cells will be considered more valuable to the organization. Should this occur, a subtle hierarchy may reemerge. This is entirely possible, given a history of socialization that suggests that "certain" differences make more of a difference than others. This is less likely to occur in the framework of the model, since it is not a hierarchy of control.

Individuals at the upper right are not "better" than individuals who are at other places in the model (organization).

The functions at the right of the model are not "control" functions or "higher order" functions in the sense of containing more responsibility or more influence over other functions. Particular care must be taken in the design to prevent this "nestedness" from evolving into a hierarchical arrangement.

HELIX MODEL

The Helix Model is another way to view an organization in very broad-based terms. Represented in Figure 7-5, it bears its name because of its obvious similarity to cellular biology.

The Helix Model illustrates that there are other ways of designing an organization than the pyramid. It contains a variety of functional links with other organizational components as well as with subsystems within and outside of the organization, including the larger culture within which the organization functions.

It attempts to portray the interrelationships among functions differently. It could also be thought of as representing a single department or one of the cells from the interactive functional responsibility chart (Figure 7-4).

STRONG PREFERENCE MODEL

The strong preference model has been used effectively as a decision-making model in both an organizational and an interpersonal context. It is built on the assumption that much of the conflict emerging within groups and between individuals is based on a power struggle rather than an actual difference in personal preference in a given situation. The strong preference proposes that individuals indicate if they have a *strong* preference for a particular option or if they have a preference only that a decision be made but not necessarily caring *what* that decision is. In the latter case, the individual may also have a strong preference that a particular outcome is not desirable.

This patterned way of interacting facilitates identification of the important (from the participant's perspective) issues and conflict points. The likelihood is greater that the real issues will emerge, rather than superficial ones based more on power acquisition than problem solving.

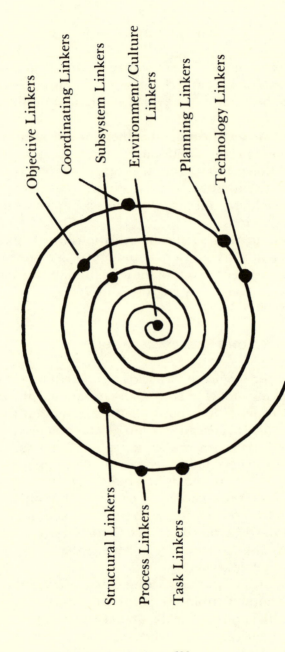

Figure 7-5   Helix Model

Objective Linkers

Coordinating Linkers

Subsystem Linkers

Environment/Culture Linkers

Planning Linkers

Technology Linkers

Structural Linkers

Process Linkers

Task Linkers

186

This model is a process as well as a structural component in a collaborative organization. It is a structure that provides a patterned form of interaction, and it is a process that indicates how to interact at organizational and interpersonal levels. It does not address or resolve the conflict that characterizes current organizational structures and processes; however, it does offer a method by which to begin to resolve conflicts and make decisions.

SEPARATION OF INCOME FROM WORK

There are several authors who suggest that, while collaboration is indeed an appropriate value and goal state toward which to strive, it is not likely that it will be achieved without a separation of income from work (Morrow and Thayer, 1977; Thayer, 1973)

Morrow and Thayer (1977) argue that while there are many contemporary authors who stress humanism, it is not likely to flourish until society devalues materialism.

> We suggest that nothing of significance can be attained until "work," however defined, is totally separated from "income." This separation, which cannot in our view be delayed much longer, must be global in scope. It follows that the separation of work from income would remove any justification for differentials in income based upon the quality and/or quantity of work performed, and also would remove the clearest distinction between superiors (those paid more) and subordinates (those paid less). (p. 449)

Morrow and Thayer review the work and theories of several prominent scholars including Rawls (1971), MacPherson, (1973) Maslow (1970), Herzberg (1966), Scott (1974), and Fromm (1976) to indicate that there are a variety of perspectives about humanism, but none will work unless the ethic of materialism is discarded.

Morrow and Thayer are correct to the extent that none of the current theories are adequate for supporting major change in current organizations — not because of a conflict between humanism and materialism, but because none of these current theories goes far enough in acknowledging the impact of hierarchy on the behavior of individuals.

Linking income to work is not really at issue; the hierarchical arrangement of work creates the problem.

Further, it is, the competition that is nourished by hierarchical authority that has emerged from vertical differentiation in organizations. The confusing messages received by individuals when a large number have "ultimate responsibility," yet no one really seems to have it, is another problem. Each claims that the responsibility is really somebody else's, that they were just "following orders" or "doing what they were told."

Morrow and Thayer (1977) also state that according to Maslow and Herzberg, materialism and humanism can be combined, while Rawls, MacPherson, Scott, and Fromm imply that there are fundamental contradictions in our current views of organizations that might be called "humanism."

Income cannot be completely separated from work; however, the elimination of the superior/subordinate dichotomy is clearly a step that must be taken if the move toward humanism or toward collaborative organizations is to be successful.

Each of the authors discussed by Morrow and Thayer postulate a dichotomy existing in the current world view as applied to organizations. Rawls (1971) uses utilitarianism-versus-justice as fairness; MacPherson (1973) pits maximizing utilities against maximizing power; Maslow (1970) uses overcoming deficiencies and self-actualization; Herzberg (1966) supports the theories of hygiene motivation; Scott (1974) has materialism with organizational humanism; and Fromm (1976) postulates "To Have" versus "To Be."

The question is no longer *whether* but rather *how* these discrepant views of the world and organizations can be resolved. These are false dichotomies, implying that neither can be part of the other.

Both ends of these continuums can be combined in the collaborative organizations and frameworks. Of course, hierrarchy must be eliminated in order for these to be considered something other than mutually exclusive variables anchoring two ends of a continuum. They emerge as anchor points only when played in the context of hierarchical organizations where competition is the dominant behavior pattern and value system.

The elimination of hierarchy and competition must take precedence over the separation of income from work, as the two variables cause a dichotomy. It is not the postulated anchor points that are incorrect; it is the conclusion drawn by Morrow and Thayer, that in order to resolve these seeming inconsistencies, income must be separated from work. In reality, the reward system must reward different things, and the context within which this reward system functions must be completely revised.

NEGOTIATED ORDER

Trist originated the phrase negotiated order, and it seems appropriate to return to it at the completion of the chapter on collaborative organizational structure. It might be better termed *renegotiated order*. This renegotiation involves functionalism and generalism rather than hierarchical authority and competition. It also involves a great deal of interdependence between task, structure, and process, with rewards given for an increased ability to function in more complex and interdependent situations.

It results in a continuous process of renegotiation and reformulation, with little reliance on one individual's "ultimate responsibility." It is a negotiated order between individuals, groups, and the larger context within which these entities flourish. It is an optimistic view of the potential of individuals and individuals impacted by systems.

The collaborative model, as it relates to organizational-structural variables, eliminates the need for over-control, and increases the probability that production, income, individuals, and work can survive elegantly in the same context.

Chapter 8

COLLABORATIVE ORGANIZATIONAL PROCESSES

Process is the interdependence of values and structure, which, in operation, causes certain behavior in individuals. It is "how" the group or organization interacts, or in terms used in Chapter 7, it is the "blood flowing through the veins." The "veins" comprise the structure. The task or goal of the organization becomes what is to be accomplished, the structure becomes the context, and the process becomes the method of achieving goals.

COMPETITIVE AND COLLABORATIVE PROCESSES IN ORGANIZATIONS

The processes of interaction in a competitive system differ greatly from those in a collaborative system. The two are more mutually exclusive than compatible in nature. As illustrated in Figure 8-1, a competitive system ties conflict to

Figure 8-1   Processes in a Competitive and Collaborative System

	In a Competitive System ...	*In a Collaborative System ...*
When	1. *Conflict* is tied to hierarchy.	1. *Conflict* is rooted in *legitimate differences.*
These Dynamics	2. *Control* is gained at other's expense (assumes fixed power pie). *Mastery* is never gained.	2. *Control* and *mastery* are gained at other's expense (unlimited power pie.)
Result In	3. Individual and group boundary permeability decreasing.	3. Individual and group boundary permeability increasing. Differences are incorporated.
Which Leads To and Results In	4. Indivduals *protect* self and *perpetuate* hierarchy.	4. Self as a given; individuals *present* self and do not respond to hierarchy.
This Happens Because	5. Someone outside the individual determines what needs are and how they will be satisfied. This is *External Control.*	5. Individual determines what needs will be satisfied, and how this will happen. This is *Internal Control.*
And Results In	6. Feeling of being *out of control* of self and organizational environment; need to control others increases as a way of gaining self-control.	6. Feelings of *mastery* and *control* of self and organizational environment increase; need to control others decreases.

Which Leads To	7. *Alienation.* Reinforcement that *conflict* is *based in* and *resolved by* the hierarchy.	7. *Commitment, involvement,* and *investment* in organization. Reinforcement that conflict is based in *legitimate differences,* and is *resolved* outside the hierarchical system.
Then To	8. *Frustration.*	8. *Problem-solving* rather than perpetuation of conflict.
And	9. *Aggression.*	9. *Awareness, creativity,* and *excitement.*
And Thus	10. *Passive-aggressive* behavior pattern— all behavior is in *response* to control and authority and resolution of these dynamics in formal organization. Risk taking is calculated.	10. *Interactive behavior pattern. Interdependence* is supported and rewarded. Risk taking is valued.
Once Again	11. Return to 1.	11. Return to 1.

hierarchy. It emerges as competition for perceived scarce resources of status, prestige, and power.

At this point, the conflict is already firmly rooted in competition. Control (winning, or at least not losing) is gained at someone else's expense with individuals operating on the basis of a fixed power structure.

Individuals and groups never gain *mastery* of skill or task completion, but are readily gaining mastery over the processes necessary for power acquisition and the perpetuation of dominance. Individuals and groups begin to draw further apart and see less in common with each other. In other words, individual and group boundary permeability decreases while individual differences heighten.

Individuals protect themselves and their power to move toward a position that minimizes losses. A hierarchical arrangement of authority is perpetuated because someone *outside of the individual* determines what needs and task priorities are important. *External control* is being imposed on the individual; at the same time, *internal control* from the individual or the task diminishes. Individuals and groups accumulate feelings of being *out of control* with regard to their perceived impact on others.

The need to control (influence) others increases as a mechanism for gaining self-control. This leads to *alienation* from each other, from subgroups, and from the very system that is nurtured by the attempts at gaining self-control.

The perception that conflict is not only rooted in hierarchy, but also is resolved only by manipulation of and interaction with this systematic arrangement of relationships, is reinforced.

This chain of events often leads to frustration and even outright aggression, such aggression usually taking the form of *passive-aggressive* behavior patterns. These behavior patterns are not characterized by outright aggression, but rather by more passive methods of "foot dragging," "time stretching," and continual "review" mechanisms designed to slow the system and move it toward a more containable format.

The predominant behavior pattern is *reactive* in character, responding to control, authority and the resolution of these dynamics in ways that are advantageous to individuals attempting to survive elegantly in formal organizations. Risk taking may occur, but it is a highly calculated procedure designed to minimize personal loss of power and control. Above all, the "place" that one occupies in the hierarchy must be maintained at all costs. The cycle is in fact a continuous process occurring simultaneously around a variety of issues at any given time for any given individual.

Processes in a Collaborative Organization

In a collaborative organization, conflict is perceived to have its origin in legitimate *individual* differences (see Figure 8-1). It is not a function of *system perpetuation*; rather, it is a function of system and individual enhancement and task accomplishment. Control and mastery are not gained at the expense of others (there is enough to go around; in fact, since functional dispersal is a goal, this is much less of an issue than in a competitive process). Individual and group boundary permeability increase. Differences provide variety and expertise rather than the threat of control. Differences are incorporated in the sense that they are included and respected, and the process, task, and structure are modified to respond to them.

In a collaborative process, the "self" is a given. Individuals feel free to *present* this complex and peculiar self openly to the organization. The individual perspective is preserved and the hierarchical arrangement is not a valid source of authority. Individuals have more input in determining what needs will be satisfied, and in the mechanisms that will be used to achieve satisfaction. Thus individuals have a larger reservoir of feelings of *internal* control and increased feelings of *mastery*, as well as control, over the organizational environment. It is also an increase in influence over the organization and system within which one functions.

These processes result in *commitment, involvement,* and *investment* in task outcomes. Individuals get reinforcement for believing that conflict is caused by legitimate individual differences and resolved without resorting to a hierarchical authority arrangement. A problem-solving approach to conflict resolution with increased individual *awareness, excitement,* and *creativity* is also a by-product of collaborative processes.

Collaborative processes also lead to *interactive* behavior patterns where *interdependence* is the normative perspective. This interdependence is rewarded and consistent with the context of the organization. Risk taking is valued and rewarded as a consistent organizational process.

Collaborative processes are cyclical in nature. They are ongoing and self perpetuating if consistent reward systems are applied to encourage appropriate behavior. These processes may decrease the current misuse of individual skills. Increased application may well result in increased productivity without expense to the individual.

COMPETITION AS COUNTERFEIT BEHAVIOR

Competition and competitive processes are counterfeit; they are not "real" behaviors; they are not the appropriate behavior patterns nor processes that increase task completion, performance, and productivity in organizations.

Competition is not good for individuals, nor for organizations, because it furthers assumptions inaccurate for individuals and not sophisticated enough for organizations as social systems. Competition only minimally enhances performance. It does not encourage investment, commitment, or support for the organization's productivity. It perpetuates survival of the current state of functioning, but it does not support change. It supports power maintenance and game playing by all the current rules instead of examining these rules or the nature of the game itself.

The behaviors that are *not* encouraged by competition are the same behaviors that the organization says it wants in its rhetoric about how it feels about its employees. Competition is counterfeit because it does the opposite of what is supposedly valued in organizations. It does little for individual improvement or self-actualization, and it does little to increase the productivity curve for the organization.

If competition is counterfeit behavior, then so is hierarchical structure counterfeit. It makes competition the primary mode of functioning in the organization. It is self-perpetuating rather than expansion oriented.

Individuals learn the "rules" of the game of power acquisition and perpetuation rather than the "rules" of task effectiveness and performance. They learn to cope with the structure rather than to manage it or to confront it. They learn how to adapt to the structure as it is, but they do not learn (or are not reinforced for) modification of the system for increasing output.

They are willing to support modification as long as their power and influence are not diminished, and as long as they are still able to understand the mechanisms necessary for this perpetuation. Understanding is necessary "up front" before the change will be supported. Individuals who are trying to survive elegantly in the organization are unlikely to support a change unless they know beforehand exactly what the change means for their power base and their ability to influence the modified system.

This is consistent with a major aim of organizations to survive at all costs, but it is not consistent with the needs to increase performance and productivity while at the same time increasing commitment and investment of employees.

Competitive processes result in a mutually exclusive set of relationships between organizational survival and employee performance. Collaborative processes do not. The latter, then, are not counterfeit in that they are consistent with both the avowed aims of organizations and the needs of individuals within that organizational system.

In fact, the collaborative process facilitates breaking away from dichotomous thinking and concepts of individuals in the context of organizations. It allows a view of structure and process as inexorably intertwined; it also facilitates a conceptual framework wherein individuals are seen as the ultimate implementors of that behavior emerging from interactions between the structure, process, task, and individual.

It departs from a dichotomous perspective of the individual and the organization; the structure and the process; the input and the output.

Collaborative processes are more consistent with systems' perspectives and contingency theories, which are much more accurate in providing understanding, not only regarding "what" happens in organizations, but also about "why" these things happen.

ORGANIZATIONAL PLURALISM

Collaborative processes stem largely from the concept of pluralism. Pluralism is an often touted value, and an often unrecognized component of many processes at both the organizational and national level. Pluralism connotes more than one "ultimate" reality, with the notion that there are a variety of perfectly appropriate perspectives given a particular set of circumstances. It is consistent with a systems approach to the understanding of organizations as well as a contingency perspective on organizational functioning.

> The capacity to accept the greater degree of pluralism that is characterizing the transition to postindustrialism and which involves loss of paramountcy in any one value or "figural" societal system will be a function of the extent to which a unifying ground can be established. (Trist, 1976, p. 1024)

This unifying ground suggested by Trist can be found in collaborative processes in organizations, as well as in the components of collaborative structures in the values necessary for a collaborative organization to work.

There is not one "best" process or one "best" structure

or value that is "correct" in all situations. The concept of a "unifying ground" is still useful since it implies certain linkings of all the variables in organizational contexts. It provides a consistent set of parameters to link values, tasks, structure and process. It is the unifying thread that allows further movement in the direction of pluralistic organizations.

At the same time that collaboration allows a move toward pluralism, pluralism accommodates a move toward collaboration. The critical point here is that there is no one best or inherently more correct way to accomplish a particular purpose or task.

There are a variety of methodologies, structures, and processes that might be linked together to form an approach for a specific situation. Pluralism is at the center of this approach, and is consistent with the collaborative perspective.

The collaborative process provides some parameters for operating in a variety of different situations rather than an exact pattern for all situations. It is rather like a road map that shows the interstate system but does not fill in all of the secondary roads. The interstate system provides the major parameters for arriving at a destination, but the secondary roads are necessary to get to the primary roads, and provide infinite variety, depending on the ultimate destination and the processes that one selects to arrive at that destination.

There is no one best way to travel to the destination, but there are some parameters for that destination that influence the infinite variety of actual paths that may be taken.

PLANNING AS A PROCESS

In an organization utilizing collaborative processes, planning would be seen and implemented primarily as a process rather than primarily as an outcome. That is not to imply that there are no outcome components to the planning process, but rather that the critical elements are those contained within the process rather than those contained within the outcomes.

Most managers (and students of the management process, as well) assume that planning is a totally rational, scientific, or highly technical process. This perspective is based on two assumptions:

1. That there was once a steady state and that there will again be another steady state. The way to get from the first to the second is to produce a complete plan which supposes that the principal future states of the system can be foreseen. (Trist, 1976, p. 1026)
2. That the implementation can be carried out with resources completely under one's own control. (Trist, 1976, p. 1026)

The outcomes of a planning process are secondary components to the process itself. Too many managers make the grave mistake of assuming that, because they have a "plan" or some goals or objectives, they have attained an appropriate outcome as a result of the planning process. Nothing could be further from the truth.

The outcomes will eventually be meaningless if the process was not an appropriate one. Future outcomes are easy to develop. Implementation creates the difficulty. A process that is involving, and that creates investment on the part of individuals who will have to implement it, has a much higher probability of succeeding than does one that has been "laid on" from above. A collaborative process that is not competitively or hierarchically oriented is more appropriate than is one oriented around competition, winning and losing, and power perpetuation and maintenance.

Trist (1976) has identified two assumptions commonly

held about the planning process. One of them revolves around the notion that there is some *exact* future that can be understood and planned. In a collaborative process, the future is not necessarily an extrapolated view of the present; it cannot be *exactly* planned for, nor can all the parameters of that future be accurately predicted in the present. Planning must be regarded as a process that supports tolerance for ambiguity and focuses on implementation elements rather than on outcome elements.

The planning processes in this framework have more of an action research focus than an outcome focus. They should be viewed as stimuli and data gathering mechanisms rather than as definitive outcome-oriented mechanisms. They should be contingency and situationally based, rather than static mechanistically oriented. They should have a heavy emphasis on the "how" of the outcome, rather than solely on the outcome itself. They should also have as their major "outcome" an exciting, creative, involving process with an emphasis on implementation.

Trist's second assumption about the planning process involves the erroneous premise that implementation can be carried out alone, or at least that one individual or a small group of individuals can implement something based on the resources they control. Nothing could be further from the truth! Implementation, almost by definition, requires others. Deciding (planning) is easy; implementation, on the other hand, requires investment, commitment, or at the very least, willingness on the part of the implementors to pay the "costs" of the implementation.

The world and the organizations functioning within that world are too complicated and too interactive and interdependent in a complex society to assume that a "plan" can be implemented on one entity's resources alone.

How does one increase the resources available for implementation? One answer is to get the implementors involved in the planning process. Involvement increases the probability of support; and support of the outcome is necessary if the "plan" is to be anything more than a "plan."

A collaborative process requires involvement in the task, structure, and process as the integrating or unifying thread throughout the entire conceptual framework. It is a movement away from outcome as the primary component, and a movement toward an interaction and interdependence between outcome and process.

CURRENT COLLABORATIVE BEGINNINGS

There are several theorists who have proposed models or modifications of models that are based on collaborative processes. These include Vroom and Yetton (1973), Eiseman (1977), and Finch (1977). Vroom and Yetton have identified a contingency model of decision making with five different models of decision making: two authoritative styles, AI and AII; two consultative styles, CI and CII; and one group style, GII. The Vroom and Yetton models are consistent with a collaborative decision making model in that one of the major variables that encourages acceptance of a particular style has to do with the implementation of the decision by others. While there are seven diagnostic questions that a manager needs to answer before he/she decides upon a particular decision making style, the issue of implementation remains a critical one in this choice of styles.

If the decision must be accepted by subordinates in order to be implemented, and if subordinates are not likely to accept it if the manager makes it, then the quality of the decision is raised considerably if the subordinates are actively involved in the decision making process *via* a group decision making model. While this model is still based on the superior-subordinate framework, it offers a glimpse into a process for decision making that is consistent with collaborative processes in organizations.

Eiseman (1977) offers a model based primarily on Walton's (1969) model of conflict resolution. While Eiseman does not deal with the context of an organization, he does offer a method of resolving conflicts in a collaborative fashion. He relies heavily on a value base of a third party to facilitate the conflict, but at least that much is recognized as critical to conflict resolution.

Fred Finch (1977) offers some exciting perspectives on collaborative leadership processes. He builds and expands from many of the current theories on leadership, most recently those of Hersey and Blanchard (1977). Finch clearly articulates the need for a divesting of power and authority on the part of the manager, and a rearrangement, if not elimination, of the traditional hierarchical and authority-based models for organizational functioning. Finch argues convincingly for a movement away from the traditional role of the manager.

> The change of the focus of the managerial role to the management of the interdependencies in organizations is an enabling change. It enables work-groups to work collaboratively because they have the power to make decisions with respect to how work gets done. Similarly, the role of the manager changes from a hierarchical to a collaborative role. The role requires dual representation—representing the workgroup to the organization and the larger organization to the workgroup. It becomes more of a facilitative, advising and negotiating role, a role that will offer new challenges and require very different values and skills. (p. 300)

The concept of the manager as a facilitator rather than a perpetuator of authority compliments the notion of collaborative leadership as a process, not a static, authority-based form of interaction and interfacing, both between the manager and the work group, and between the manager and the rest of the organization, i.e., other facilitators, other work groups, and other organizational processes.

Argyris and Schon (1978) have discussed a collaboratively based model for functioning organizations. This is an extension and application of Argyris's earlier work on Model I and Model II approaches to organizations. Clearly Model II is exemplary of collaborative processes in organizations. It clearly recognizes the need to rethink drastically and formulate thoughts about the place of hierarchical and competitively-based models for organizational functioning.

PROBLEM FINDING LINKED TO PROBLEM SOLVING

Ingalls (1976) has separated the problem finding process from the problem solving process. He has indicated that different levels of internal states, as well as different behavior patterns, are appropriate for both problem finding and problem solving.

Problem finding, or problem identification as it is often called, lends itself more readily to tolerance for ambiguity, interpersonal relationships, intuition, and emotion. Once the problem has been "found," then object relations (I-it) and certainty accompanied by sensation and thought are more appropriate.

This breakdown of problem solving into two more distinct processes, each having appropriate accompanying conditions, conforms to the collaborative process.

In the same way that objectives need to be linked, so do processes need to be linked in a systematic fashion. Individuals who are a part of a variety of processes are likely to see and feel the disparities between processes more quickly than those who are influencing *outside* of the process.

Since the process of objective setting is inextricably tied to the processes of objective implementation, these ties must be examined by a manager to be sure that they are internally consistent, and to be sure that contradictory or mutually exclusive processes have not been inadvertently established.

WORKER AND MANAGER GOALS

It should be quite clear by now that the individuals usually labeled workers and those usually labeled managers have virtually the same goals in a collaborative organization. They probably have the same goals in a competitive organization, with the exception that they seldom realize that each functions within different contexts and processes and thus works toward achieving those goals differently.

Both groups wish to be competent and to be seen as such; they both wish to be productive and to be seen as such; and they also have a strong desire to have control over their lives and destinies in the organization. They are ready and able to learn and to exhibit mastery over particular tasks, structures, and processes. They wish to have that capability primarily within their own control rather than outside in someone else's control.

Various subgroups or status levels are closer together than it appears if one looks at the organizational arrangements within which each group functions. Their respective behavior and value systems are much more attributable to the nature of the organization than they are to some inherent differences within individual human beings. Collaborative processes recognize this assumption and are formulated and implemented accordingly.

FUNCTIONAL DISPERSAL INDEX

Current organizational functioning and traditional management roles are often associated with the maxims, "Develop your people" or "Bring your people along."

While this may be freely given advice, or a perfectly appropriate expectation, the managers to whom this advice is given are often at a loss to know exactly how to behave in order to respond. The typical response is to become more authoritarian, more watchful, and more concerned with making sure that he/she (the manager) and his/her good reputation as management potential are not lost in the shuffle.

Functional dispersal asserts (Chapter 7) that functions, or ways of doing things, are to be spread out, or disbursed, to as great a variety of individuals as possible. It is assumed that some individuals will be willing and able to assume a great variety of functions, while others will opt for a smaller amount, both in quantity and complexity. One of the possible criterion leading to differential reward, therefore, is an index of the functional dispersal level at which a particular person is working.

If the task and process are highly complex, and if the structure is highly interdependent, then the individual would have a high functional dispersal index, and he/she would be high on the developmental reward path (Chapter 7). This index might also include a measure of the degree to which certain individuals are assisting others to increase their functional disbursement level.

This type of index is consistent with some of the recent thinking and writing on job design, which emphasizes increasing the job characteristics of autonomy and feedback, as well as skill variety and task significance. It is also parallel with the notions of job enrichment in its most "ideal" form. It clearly faces a reorientation of power distribution and results in vastly different opinions of authority. This index presupposes a more egalitarian perspective, but it attempts to recognize and respond to individual differences in both skill and interest level.

POWER IN ORGANIZATIONS

The use of power and control in organizations is one of the most critical components in system functioning. It has only recently been examined systematically as a central factor in alternative organizational structures and processes. Slater (1970) comments:

> Nothing is poisonous if taken in small enough quantities, and the more power is diffused the more the assumption of power looks like the assumption of responsibility. It is when power is concentrated that the pursuit of it takes on an unhealthy hue. (p. 47)

A collaborative framework for power is not one that designates power as an unimportant variable. Power diffusion, not power elimination, is the focus here, as the relationship of hierarchical structures to the perpetuation of power concentration is examined.

Expertise is seen, in competitive organizations, as a result of one's horizontal level in the hierarchy rather than from a functional perspective.

The assumptions that one acts upon in relation to the amount of power available in the organizational system are crucial to the further understanding of hierarchical organizations. The nesting characteristic of hierarchy reinforces the notion that the amount of power is limited by the nature of the organization (fixed power pie).

As soon as one acts on this assumption, the Pygmalion effect begins to operate. Because one acts as if power is limited, the organization (nesting) reinforces this; the fact that it began as an assumption or value system (competition) becomes unimportant. Individuals behave competitively to gain a share of the perceived limited supply of power and control, the hierarchical structure acts in a rewarding fashion, and the individual "learns" that competition for limited power is an appropriate behavior pattern.

REVIEW OF POWER LITERATURE

A great many theorists have categorized and classified some of the various ways individuals try to influence each other. Filley and House (1969) list several of these:

Russel (1938): Rewards and punishments, physical power, influence on opinion.

Bierstedt (1950): Control of money, knowledge, competence, prestige, deceit, fraud, secrecy, power through organization, power by numbers, control of property.

Simon (1957): Legitimacy, rewards and sanctions, confidence, social approval.

French and Raven (1959): Legitimate power, rewards, expertise, reference power, cohesive power.

Presthus (1960): Deference to authority and formal position, expertise, rapport.

Gillman (1962): Authority, cohesion, persuasion, manipulation.

Cartwright (1965): Legitimate power, control over gains and costs, control of information, personal affection, physical control.

Swingle (1976) has written about the management of power in organizations in a very applied fashion. He discusses the dynamics of power and their application in a variety of formats, but he does not question the source of power perpetuation and the reasons for its primacy in organizational contexts.

Thompson (1967) raises the issue that power might possibly be based on interdependence. He suggests that power dependence allows one to consider power from other than a zero-sum perspective (Emerson, 1962; Parsons, 1960). Thompson states:

> By considering power in the context of interdependence, we admit the possibility of A and B becoming increasingly powerful with regard to each other—the possibility that increasing interdependence may result in increased net power. (p. 32)

Thompson is one of the few theorists who seriously considers the increase of power that both parties might accrue if they are functioning in an interdependent fashion. While Thompson does not build his entire case upon this consideration, he includes it in his discussion of organizations. He also considers it in terms of the competition that may exist in interorganizational competition.

Slater (1974) discusses two kinds of power—positive power and negative power. While perhaps a bit oversimplified and too strongly stated, he says that "negative power is the ability to control, force, imprison, invade, terrify, and kill others" (p. 123).

Positive power, on the other hand, "is the ability to influence others, to arouse love and respect, and to get one's needs met—without pressure and in a socially naked and unadorned state, devoid of status, position, or other weaponry" (p. 123).

Positive power is applicable to the uses of power in a collaboratively functioning organization, for while power does exist in a collaborative organization, it exists and functions in a *very different, in fact, revolutionary way.* Collaborative organizations would concentrate not on the elimination of power but on its *equalization* and *disbursement.*

Saul Alinsky (1972) has some very strong and poignant strategies for changing organizations and cultural systems, which are clearly based on power as a critical variable both in understanding the current functioning of organizations and in selecting strategies to change these systems.

Power is not static; it cannot be frozen and preserved like food; it must grow or die. Therefore, in order to keep power the status quo must get more. But from whom? There is just so much more that can be squeezed out of the Have-Nots—so the Haves must take it from each other. They are on a road from which there is no turning back. This power cannibalism of the Haves permits only temporary truces, and only when equally confronted by a common enemy. Even then there are regular breaks in the ranks, as individual units attempt to exploit the general threat for their own special benefit. Here is the vulnerable belly of the status quo. (p. 149)

Alinsky's strategies have a great deal of short range viability. However, their long range applicability for organizational change is questionable. While they match the current state of organizational functioning, they also end up perpetuating the current systems. Even so, Alinsky provides insight into the current state of organizational functioning. He is quite clear about the system's attempts to perpetuate itself and is also clear about the dynamics that are likely to emerge in this process. In their attempts to gather or regather the power for themselves, individuals respond to the threat of power. In a competitive struggle (which a change effort often is) each of the parties struggles to minimize the losses. Any gains are made at someone else's expense. This is most probably true in a hierarchical structure with a competitive behavior pattern and a perception of zero-sum dynamics regarding power.

SECRECY AND POWER

One of the clearest examples of power perpetuation in hierarchical organizations is the need for secrecy of information. Information leads to increased power; thus, hiding information or keeping it secret, or only releasing portions, leads to increased need for the person who holds the remainder of the information to remain in his/her current position. "The ability to maintain a permanent concentration of power depends upon the ability to maintain and enforce secrecy and dispersal tends to follow automatically . . . upon breakdown of this ability" (Slater, 1970, p. 145).

One of the ways to begin to change the nature of organizational power perpetuation is to make information more available to a larger number of individuals; to make decision making processes more open, more organic, more consensual in nature.

This creates a great deal of resistance on the part of individuals at a variety of levels in the organization. It means a reduced elitism, which results from a strong vertical differentiation in organizational structure. It is not consistent with efforts to strengthen "professional" managers, but clearly results in greater power disbursement.

> Every bureaucracy seeks to increase the superiority of the professionally informed by keeping their knowledge and intentions secret. Bureaucratic administration always tends to be an administration of "secret sessions"; in so far as it can, it hides its knowledge and action from criticism. (Weber, 1946, p. 38)

INTERACTION OF HIERARCHY AND POWER

Most organizations in Western society function within the confines of a hierarchy, and thus promote competition. Hierarchy encompasses both differentiated *functions* and differentiated *authority*. Hierarchical organizations contain a division of labor as a horizontal "cut" of the organization, and use the vertical "cut" of the organization to indicate differential authority levels. While Level B (Figure 8-2) may perform a different function than Level C and may indicate differential functions at both horizontal and vertical levels, this is unlikely because of the *nesting* characteristic of hierarchy.

Nesting presupposes that one level can be completely subsumed by or incorporated into the level above it, and that it completely incorporates the level below it. The analogy of a telescoping pole portrays the encompassing nature of the nesting process. While the pole may be "opened up" for some uses, the fact that it can be "closed up" so that some

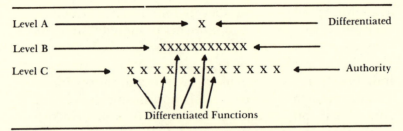

Figure 8-2   Hierarchy with Differentiated Functions and Authority as well as Nesting

portions or sections completely disappear places severe boundaries and constraints on the nature of the pole (system).

"Lower" levels have potential to be incorporated into "upper" levels, but "upper" levels have "responsibility" for "lower" levels. The responsibility emerges as a characteristic of the nesting process and results in differential authority.

Upper levels are designed to have a greater or more encompassing responsibility. A series of interactions emerges whereby differentiated authority becomes intertwined with differentiated functions. What began as a clear separation of functions results in an overriding of differential functions by differential authority.

Authority roles become paramount over functional roles. This is consistent with the hierarchical structure's nesting characteristic. Competition for perpetuation of the nesting character of the structure evolves as naturally as if it were carefully planned.

FIXED POWER PIE

The perception of a fixed power pie is one held by individuals who behave in ways to get as much of it as they possibly can.

Competition for perceived scarce resources of power and status as well as prestige and influence constitute a survival mechanism to guarantee that one receives his/her share of the "spoils" of organizational life. The major element illustrative of this is the belief that there is only so much power to go around. As long as one believes this, and acts accordingly, there *will* be only so much to go around! If a large number of players hold this belief, it will become a self-fulfilling prophecy.

Individuals do things to ensure that they won't lose the power or influence they already possess. They behave in ways to prevent others from winning, especially if they can't win. As long as everyone is acting under the impression that power is not a relationship, this behavior works. However, a relationship does exist, and it takes two to keep the relationship active and productive (productive in the sense that it works for one of the parties involved).

As long as individuals are unaware of the assumptions on which they are acting, or as long as the organizational structures and processes are such that power acquisition, perpetuation, and retention (at another's expense) are perfectly legitimate, these processes and dynamics will continue to flourish in high style.

STRATEGIES OF CONFLICT RESOLUTION

The behavioral science and management literature lists three major processes for conflict resolution in organizations:

1. Win-Lose Methods;
2. Negotiation Methods; and
3. Problem Solving

Win-lose methodologies are very common when one individual or department possesses "all the marbles" and is sure he/she or it can "win." It is the strategy of "lining up your ducks" for the big battle. It's a great strategy for the winner, but not so great for the loser. It's also not so great for the winner if he/she has to work with the losing individual or department again. Losers don't forget!

Negotiation strategies are often used when neither party believes that it can get all it wants. In order to avoid a total loss, the parties negotiate or compromise. Like the win-lose strategy, negotiation concerns itself with all of the usual dynamics of hierarchical and competitive organizations. It is a strategy that is most consistent with the expectations of power acquisition and perpetuation, and results in alliances of a temporary nature, which are useful while they last. As the balance of power changes, however, these alliances break down. Negotiation is a short term strategy with short term benefits and long term difficulties.

Problem solving strategies require quite a different set of assumptions and behavior patterns. These strategies are not as consistent with the mainstream expectations of the organization in that they require trust, openness, and a willingness and ability to reexamine and redefine the problem. Problem solving involves an expectation that both parties involved can get what they want, that each can "win." Since it is not dependent on hierarchical authority or approached with a competitive mentality, it is most consistent with a collaborative process. Problem solving is not dependent on the perpetuation of one's position, values, or position in the organization. It involves, usually, a recognition that most conflict situations are based on competition, power perpetuation, and some historical accumulation of feelings and perceptions revolving around these issues. These feelings and perceptions must be brought out into the open if there is any hope of resolution. If not, if the problem is not redefined to include these historical dynamics, or if the individuals are not willing to interact with a different set of assumptions, or if they are not willing to take the risks involved in this methodology, then the negotiation methodology, or the win-lose methodology, will probably be used. The causes of the conflict will not really be examined by negotiation or win-lose strategies. The individuals or department will not be dealing with conflict, they will only be responding to it.

The conflict will emerge again, with some slightly different dynamics and manifestations, and it will probably be more difficult to deal with. The causes won't go away, nor will the conflict. Individuals will still respond to the hierarchical structure with competitive behavior patterns and the very problems that the conflict resolution methodology was designed to solve will occur again, and again, and again. . . .

POWER AND PERFORMANCE REVIEW

Current methods and behaviors involved in performance review reinforce the belief that there is only so much to go around. It is typical that only a certain number of individuals can receive an outstanding rating, that there can only be so many stars. This process reinforces the notion that power is fixed with only a certain amount to go around.

An alternative methodology, more consistent with a collaborative organization, has been identified. It recognizes that individual differences exist, and are carried over into an organizational context. If clear performance criteria, including task and process complexity, were in existence, as well as structural component interdependence, and if a functional disbursement index were to be *consistently* used, collaborative processes would be more realistic.

Chapter 9

COLLABORATIVE SUBSYSTEMS IN HIERARCHICAL ORGANIZATIONS

This chapter illustrates some examples of collaborative subsystems functioning in a larger hierarchical framework to show how these subsystems work in terms of individual and organizational values, as well as structure and process. Some analysis and comparison of issues and dynamics already raised are also provided.

CASE NO. 2: ELIMINATION OF COMPETITION AND CONFLICT BY ORGANIZATIONAL RESTRUCTURE

For years there had been a constant struggle between the underwriting and agency departments in Insurance Company X. (A similar case — Case No. 1 — was discussed briefly in Chapter 3.)

The conflict arose from the differences between the roles

and missions of these two departments. The agency department was charged with increasing the sales volume through developing and motivating an "agency plan," whereas the underwriting department was responsible for producing an underwriting profit.

The agency department would try to please the agents so that they would direct most of their business to Company X. The underwriting department was less concerned with pleasing agents than it was with the proper selection and pricing of the business produced by those agents.

Specific areas of conflict involved differences between the two departments as to number, location, and quality of agency appointments; rates of commission paid to agents; careful and thorough underwriting versus accommodating agents by accepting business easily; rate levels employed ("competitive" vs. "proper"); restrictive actions, such as canceling or refusing renewal of policies; payment of losses that were technically not covered, etc.

At the personal level, the vice presidents of these two departments competed for the president's favor, and jealousy and political maneuvering abounded. In the field offices, the young people in the underwriting department envied their agency department counterparts for their company cars, expense accounts and an apparent light caseload. Perceived inequities in salaries existed in both departments.

All of these conflicts were eliminated with two quick organizational changes: the two departments reorganized under the same leader, and the responsibility for the two functions was given to everyone, regardless of rank or seniority.

Specifically, upon the retirement of the underwriting vice president, his successor was put in charge of the two departments. The successor's first act was to redesign all jobs so that each person had combined responsibility for the underwriting and agency functions. Everyone was charged with "profitable growth" in the new combined Marketing Department.

The conflicting roles were eradicated, and a new process, i.e., functional disbursement, began to take shape.

CASE NO. 3: AGENCY AND UNDERWRITING DEPARTMENTS

A similar conflict (as in Case No. 2) had existed between both the old agency and underwriting departments and the administration department, which was responsible for policy processing, premium collection, and clerical services in the field offices.

The office managers of administration were charged with controlling expenses and living within tight budgetary constraints.

As a result, they were perceived as the people who cared more about cutting costs than rendering proper and necessary service to customers, agents, and the other departments, the people who said "no."

The administration manager was forced into the role of constantly refusing special requests; trying to explain clerical errors and tardy policy issuance; and arguing with agents about premium collection problems. He and his staff were always at odds with either the Underwriting or Agency groups.

This 40-year struggle and its attendant frustrations were also eliminated by a change in the structure of the organization.

The functions that the administration department performed for the new marketing department were all transferred to the new department, along with the annual and clerical personnel involved. With everyone on the same team, with common leadership and the same objectives, strife was replaced with cooperation.

CASE NO. 4: A SUBSYSTEM OF FLIGHT ATTENDANTS

Background and Setting

The subsystem is composed of a director and five managers, three of whom are middle management level and two are senior middle management level. The latter have other managers reporting to them.

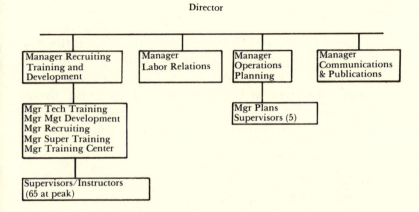

The subsystem is part of a 3,500 employee service division of a billion-dollar-a-year transportation organization. The new subsystem was created following a divisionwide organizational development effort, and has both staff and operational work objectives with an overriding objective to provide human resource management services to the four large divisional operating units.

How Collaboration Came About

In this instance, collaboration was a desirable outcome although not a part of the active plan. Two situational factors acted together to promote and to help maintain collaboration:

> —a period of unusually high, complex and novel task demands on the subsystem; and
>
> —a program in which success was achieved in incremental steps through increasingly greater collaborative efforts.

The process started with an early team-building exercise, involving the director and his immediate subordinates, and aimed at three objectives:

1. *Role and Interface Awareness.* Because this was the first real opportunity since the introduction of the new organization and new work group, exchanges were primarily concerned with clarifying prescribed and discretionary roles, as well as identification of interdependence and processes that would facilitate interdependent activities.
2. *Sharing of Expectations.*
3. *Goal Setting.* The suprasystem had embarked on a systemwide work planning and review process. Group goals, as well as a "first cut" of individual objectives, were established at these meetings.

Several weeks later, the same process was carried out at the next level by the three managers with subordinates. Because the group was relatively new and had no previous criteria for performance, it was difficult to establish the success of these exercises in contributing to effectiveness.

The processes were converted into action and the organization was much better prepared to increase the task quantity and complexity that followed (some activities increased 200% and had to be completed in the same amount of time and with almost no staff changes).

To summarize the subsystem at this stage, the director (as a former Organizational Development person) clearly supported collaboration and was in turn supported by two key subordinates, with one manager pessimistic and the two others at least willing to give it a try. The remaining management group was apparently very receptive to increased collaboration.

Crisis Leads to Increased Collaboration

Because of market opportunities, the subsystem learned of an unusually large increase in task demands, far in excess of their present staff, facilities and equipment capabilities, with little time to acquire the resources necessary to complete the task.

During the planning stage for these new demands, the director and his subordinates articulated the principle that normal hierarchical processes would be abandoned and replaced by the principle that the "task should be completed by the most expert person, regardless of position, official job role or other subordinates." This statement was followed by the following action steps:

—Task groups were organized, assigned specific goals and given a great deal of discretion as to how to attain them;

—Normal control systems were abandoned;

—Important decisions were made by all persons competent on the subject with consensus as the goal; and

—Risk taking, by the nature of the time constraints, was necessary; punishment and sanctions were seldom applied in the case of failure.

Some unanticipated behavior occurred:

—Absenteeism dropped off remarkably;

—Tardiness, previously a major problem, was no longer an issue. Most persons worked overtime on a regular basis, thus it became inappropriate to monitor tardiness;

—Office space was at a premium, and persons who required thinking time were allowed to do it at home. This expression of autonomy was probably instrumental in the internalizing of control processes;

—Group cohesiveness was very high and spilled over into nonworking hours, as socialization between group members increased dramatically; and

—The trust relationship was established with the union. Cooperation increased to the point where union members were invited as participants and observers on projects of interest that impacted union members.

Seeds of Suprasystem Concern

The group norms that were developing in the subsystem were the opposite of those in the suprasystem. Two distinct reactions were discernible:

Intradivision. The four major operations groups considered collaboration as unrealistic and faddish. There was some feeling that this type of model could lead to demands for greater autonomy and power sharing within their groups. While they attempted to do so, they could not effectively prevent collaboration because of the support given by the division vice-president. They did, however, attempt to influence those persons within the subsystem, not fully committed to collaboration, to oppose it. They also gained support, where possible, from outside the division.

Interdivision. The corporate human resource group had effective power and cooperation from all divisional human resource groups. The subsystem director, however, resisted all the attempts of the corporate human resource group to gain control, and in fact, gained a tremendous degree of autonomy from them. It was not long before participants from both groups began to stereotype each other as uncooperative, etc.

As a Collaborative Effort, Was the Subsystem Successful?

In terms of collaboration, absolutely. The experience deeply impressed a number of persons who, when gathered together, shared the memories of the experience. The great majority who have been asked whether they would repeat the experience, including the high work price that most paid, invariably answered yes. The subsystem performed all the components of its task during that one year without a hitch. Not only did participants meet the increased requirements, they produced some of the most creative efforts ever seen by the division. Most of the positive changes are still in effect today.

The other question is whether a traditional form of management could have worked as well. Were the participants responding to the crisis alone, and not to collaboration? This two-part question is more difficult to answer in the affirmative.

Based on divisional history, one could have expected the participants to have insisted on overtime payments as some would have refused to work overtime without pay. Persons might be expected to exercise their creativity outside of the work place, to be concerned only with goals that fall within their official roles, to compete for scarce resources rather than to cooperate, and finally, to resolve conflict by traditional win-lose and negotiation methods.

To speculate whether the group would have reached the objectives, it is very possible that it would have fallen short by a considerable margin in the traditional system, and that quality of work may have been proportionately less.

Pressures to Return to a Traditional Management Style Succeed

The basic reason for success in introducing collaboration was the continued removal of restraining forces. When the divisional vice-president and the subsystem director began to substitute driving forces because of environmental pressures, the support for collaboration within the subsystem decreased, and a movement toward traditional management appeared inevitable. Some of the driving forces were:

—The divisional vice-president was promoted and his replacement was given a mandate to cut costs and bring management practices "up to standard." It became very clear to subsystem members that only traditional styles of management would be rewarded. Administrative rules and regulations, as well as considerable control from the vice-president, were also aimed at discouraging participative management. The dissidence grew, the traditional style managers resurfaced, and the resolve of the procollaboration managers was tested; and

—The oil crisis occurred shortly thereafter to enflame the driving forces further.

The subsystem director began to believe that he was fighting a losing battle and would hurt his career in the process. He became involved in conflict with his two staunchest supporters of collaboration. One issue arose out of a disagreement over performance evaluation, which developed into a win-lose conflict (the subordinate lost and transferred out of the organization).

The other issue involved the dilemma of the director when the decision of a subordinate supposedly cost the company over $1 million in additional payments to union members. The group vice-president wanted the subordinate fired, but the issue was finally resolved when he offered his resignation.

Pressures were also building up elsewhere. The group had earned a reputation for being the "last of the big spenders," for being isolationists and uncooperative. Much of this label could be traced to the corporate personnel group and, to a lesser extent, to the division operating groups. The new division vice-president seemed to be firmly committed to compliance with suprasystem norms and to compliance with corporate personnel guidelines. When the subsystem lacked internal and external support, there was no resistance. Within a very short period of time, the two managers were replaced with genuine and recognized traditionalists, and the organization resumed operation consistent with a traditional model. It remains so today.

CASE NO. 5: A SOCIAL STUDIES DEPARTMENT

Place: This case takes place in a small southeast Ohio town (26,000 population) with a major university within its boundaries (24,000 students). The local high school (grades 9-12) had a new physical plant built in 1968. The high school was constructed with some new educational methods in mind — modular scheduling, phasing (student selected ability grouping), nongrading (classes might have 9th and 12th grades in the same class).

The 1,200 students took courses from these major departments — social studies, English, math, science, business, humanities/art/music, physical education, industrial arts. All of these were multiperson departments and each had a chairperson.

Subject: The social studies team consisted of nine full-time faculty, all but one of whom taught social studies for their entire class load. One taught French and social studies.

Eight of the nine staff members were under age 35, and seven were male. There was a chairperson who was unlimitedly responsible for the program, but who also had teaching duties.

In 1968, with a new facility, all academic programs were subject to revision. The social studies program had department goals established by nine staff members. These goals fit into the school goals set up by the administration (principal, assistant principal, superintendent) with little faculty input.

The system goals called for a three-year social studies sequence required of all students in the high school. The sequence of American history, Western civilization, and non-Western cultures meant that in any given year all students in the high school would be taking the same social studies course. The classes were also phased by difficulty (1 = remedial to 5 = most advanced). The students selected their own level.

The social studies staff was asked to write a curriculum for each year of the program — objectives for the course and each unit plus the acquisition of audiovisual materials and the assignment of readings. They were also responsible for recommending a budget for social studies and for designing schedules of classes, maintaining a resource center, providing tutoring, and designing a portable teaching space.

To accomplish these goals, the staff met on a weekly basis. Provision was made for each social studies staff member to be free at the same hour once a week. The schedule was adhered to as meeting times and were always used for critiquing and ongoing planning.

Meetings were conducted in a formal manner, led by the chair. There was an ongoing agenda of program development, with time spent to preview materials or discuss problems arising from phasing, discipline, etc. as they occurred.

All staff members had *equal power* within the group. Most were the same age, with approximately the same amount of teaching experience. One older teacher and the department head were the exceptions. Teachers could be identified by the phase/level they taught and there were subgroups by phase within the total staff.

Often, however, problems, concerns, and successes in one phase were discussed by all in the department.

All seemed committed to having the total social studies program work well, and all shared equally in required tasks. With no particular training, people listened to each other, expressed opinions and offered suggestions, and critiqued the program. Each member seemed valued by all the others and the social studies staff functioned as a unit to accomplish its tasks.

The staff took pride in its innovations of a learning resource center for social studies, created from its own space and staffed by social studies teachers who accommodated it within the confines of their own schedules.

Since all staff members had large group lectures (200–400 students), conducted traditionally sized classes (25–30), and directed small group discussions, all members supported the efforts of the others — offering suggestions of material, helping with audiovisual equipment and materials, and critiquing each large group session. The large group presentations, which occurred once a week, were a task shared by the entire department.

The department was proud of its solid program. The members added to their expertise yearly. Most of the staff worked together for two years. While several staff members left the system, no one new was added until the third year of this program. All noticed the difficulty in allowing that new person to enter and be recognized.

On the whole, there was mutual support and shared pride in accomplishments. The department head was also lavish in his praise of the program, and students were very responsive.

Although the rewards came primarily from peer support, there was recognition within the larger system. In the high school, the social studies department was one of ten other departments. However, since members dealt with almost all the students in the high school each year, they were in a favorable position in light of budget considerations and space allocations. Their schedules and those of the English department were figured first, with other departments worked around them.

In rank order, social studies and English were considered most important, followed by math, science, and others. Being connected with the social studies department carried some prestige among other faculty.

Because of its unique scheduling and presentation methods, the social studies staff was also a part of the outside school publicity in various conferences and presentations.

In the third year of the program, the social studies department chairman became the high school principal. The group then achieved both personal and system support.

CASE NO. 6: AN ACCREDITATION TEAM

The macro organization is an accrediting organization for five New England states. It has an administration in a major city, but most work is done by teachers/professors and administrators in the field. Each school or college desiring accreditation must be evaluated on a periodic basis and must pay a fee for membership. Most of the organization's work is done on site at schools and colleges by teams of educators. Each team (visiting committee) is composed of 12 to 20 people. The teams or visiting committees are the subject of this study. The teams referred to here are those that evaluate secondary/middle schools.

A school seeking accreditation or renewal of accreditation must do its own self-evaluation over a 12 to 15 month period prior to a visit by the evaluation team. The material from a school self-study is forwarded to the chairperson of the visiting committee. The chairperson is generally a principal or superintendent of a member school. He/she spends time with the principal of the target school about six months before the scheduled visit, and thus becomes familiar with the school and with the self-evaluation reports. He/she also selects the visiting committee members from names suggested by the accrediting organization. This list of visiting committee members is also approved by the principal of the target school. The chairperson makes all subcommittee assignments for the visiting committee and sets up a schedule for the 3½-day evaluation of the target school.

Team members are volunteers and are given release time from their schools, but receive no additional pay for their service. Teachers on the visiting committee chair subject area subcommittees in which they are experts, and also serve as members of one or two other committees in which their expertise is more limited.

All subject areas are represented, as well as special areas such as guidance, special education, student activities, school facilities, and administration. Subcommittees such as school and community, and school philosophy, contain members of varying academic specialties. Each visiting committee also has a member who represents the state department of education. This person also advises committee members on application and interpretation of state education statutes.

The visiting committee assembles on a Sunday afternoon, tours the building of the school to be evaluated, and gets material from the system self-evaluation. The chair of the visiting committee briefs his/her committee as to their task and checks the schedule for the 3½ days. Each subcommittee chair (of which there are 22) must write a report on his/her area and present it to the entire committee for approval.

Committee Task: Within the 3½ days, committee members must become familiar with every aspect of the target school, must do their own questioning and reading, write reports, and present them to the committee for approval. They may also be required to make revisions and resubmit a report.

Although feeling the task may be impossible, all go systematically about their work. Members who have served before help new members with appropriate questions, places to check, and the proper way to render reports. Members whose reports are not due for presentation until the second day help those with early presentations in data gathering and writing. Notices posted in a central place assist the chair and vice chair in keeping track of data gathered, suggest people to see, and keep members on schedule.

The chairpersons are usually dictatorial in their schedule maintenance. Techniques of control vary from just short of debate to running until everyone is either satisfied or exhausted. Intense concern for semantics wans by the second day.

Within the visiting committee, each subcommittee chair has his/her own area for control. Everyone's a leader and a follower. The subcommittee chairs can ask members of their committee to seek out certain people for interviews, gather data, write sections of reports, or meet at certain times. Although subcommittee chairs strongly request that some tasks be performed, everyone is willing to do whatever he/she can on other reports within the time constraints.

The chairperson or assistant chairperson is always available within the committee room to help in whatever way possible. This person also begins each day with the total committee and makes announcements, or on some occasions, chastises committee members about indiscretions. A high level of confidentiality about the material gathered and presented by the visiting committee is maintained. This material is only a portion of the data used to evaluate a school for accreditation.

The chair is the task master, and spends much time

making sure everyone is present when meetings are held, and ensures the continuity of presentations and discussions of subcommittee reports.

Much of the success of the 3½ days of evaluation depends upon the prior organization by the chair. The excellence of the product of the 3½ days depends on the commitment of the visiting committee members.

Without exception, in this particular case, the visiting committee members all accepted each other — meals were a break and were always very open and jovial. After the last meeting of the day, members volunteered to help others with their reports.

After 3½ days of intense attention to task, the visiting committee ("the enemy" in the eyes of the school staff who frequently misunderstood the goals of the visit and saw the committee as a threat to their jobs; yet the committee, in fact, makes no reference to individuals, nor does it evaluate individuals) meets with the target school staff and administration for a preliminary report by the visiting committee chair. The visiting committee leaves immediately after that presentation. The task of the visiting committee is complete. They are charged to keep their information about the target school confidential. In this case, few of the committee members gathered again, but many professed a great sense of accomplishment. As a cooperative unit they accomplished a gigantic task. There were few conflicts, all of which were resolved. All of the 22 reports were approved by consensus. A huge amount of knowledge/data was assimilated, evaluated, and reported.

The group and the experience were unique, and presented some unique dynamics. The group was formed for one specific task to be performed within a given period of time. There were times within the 3½ days of working sessions when tempers flared or people reacted to others in the group. Each time the personal issues were subverted to the task.

CASE No. 7: INTERACTION OF TECHNICAL
EXPERTISE AND COMPETITION

The data processing department in this company was decentralized by line of businesses but had one common data center to run each department's systems. It had been determined that there was a need to have as many standardized procedures as possible in order to schedule and run the various systems from each area in the most efficient way. Some of the needed standards had impact in the individual systems areas.

An area within corporate data processing (CDP), where the data center was located, was set up by CDP to develop, disseminate, and enforce needed data center standards. The area asked for — and received — representatives from each Line of Business (LOB) systems areas to participate in the research needed to develop the standards.

Responsibilities included assisting in research and determining alternatives for needed standard procedures, assessing the impact of a new standard on their individual areas, and helping to disseminate the standard once (if) approved.

The representatives were senior technical people, and they reported to the manager of the standards section for these special projects. The representatives provided input to the decision-making process, but did not make the actual decision(s) on what became the standard. That responsibility was left with the standards manager.

The process worked very well. The standard manager and representatives cooperated very effectively in appropriately assessing/determining the need for a standard procedure and the procedural components once the need was determined. Usually, conflicts of interest and/or ideas between members could be compromised and resolved with a minimum of conflict.

The collaboration within this group was very high. The thrust seemed to be in doing what was technically sound. Little or no politics entered into the business decisions made. If problems occurred, it was usually at the point of top management approval prior to implementation. Although the people with the technical expertise had collaborated to determine a sound technical/cost effective approach that all areas could live with, the managers often used the proposed standard as weapons against each other.

Each manager runs his/her own data processing operation within the line of business he/she is associated with. While there is a lot of common data processing knowledge that could be shared to benefit these managers, they generally prefer to avoid cooperation with each other. In fact, there is tremendous competition among them to gain special priority in the data center. At the same time, they are usually arguing with the data center about having to conform to data center rules.

The impact of this lack of cooperation on collaboration and on the established standards processes initially resulted in a reduction of their level of effectiveness, loss of credibility among their users, and dilution or negation of some sound technical decisions that would have improved data center efficiency and customer service. The managers used these decisions as a means to perpetuate competition and rivalry among themselves.

Over time, however, the situation has been turned around. Two major events made this possible. The standards area level of collaboration was supported by factual data, research, and cost records. There were very few instances where the recommendations did not prove to be valid.

On the other hand, almost every decision the managers forced brought negative repercussions. One of the most traumatic was a decision involving card input as data entry method for third generation systems.

The standards function was asked to develop a standard

banning the use of all card input in third generation systems by the data center. Any card input would have to be handled by remote job entry (data entry at a location other than the data center) and would be the customer's or user's responsibility.

The standards function, along with the designated system area representatives, researched the problem and recommended the following standard: Use of card input to the data center files is not permitted for third generation systems. Parameter and control card input will be allowed.

The standards group had determined that new development should utilize more state-of-the-art data entry alternatives and that sufficient remote terminal entry resources existed to handle data entry from remote locations for existing systems. Parameter and control cards would be allowed (this information was needed by the computer center operators to run the systems) until the data center developed an adequate cost effective method of handling parameters and control instructions without the use of cards.

The data center manager refused to accept the recommendation of the standards group and insisted that *absolutely no card input be used.* After months of debating the issue, the data center manager's "no-card standard" was implemented.

Problems were encountered almost immediately. The most common problems with the no-card standard was the need to convert parameter and control cards to other data entry methods. It was costing more (two to 100 times) to create noncard entries. Many systems were found to have only two to 10 parameter or control cards, and the cost of system revisions and alternative source entry far outweighed any data center benefits.

Recognizing the problem, the standards group began to administer the standard as they had originally developed it. Data center managers refused to cooperate and did not run any jobs with card input.

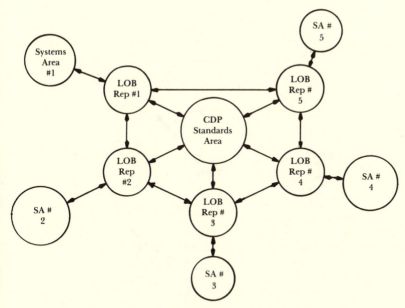

Corporate Data Processing Standards Area collaborates with
each Systems Area Rep.

Each Systems Area Rep collaborates with each other Systems
Area Rep, and with the CDPS Area, and with his/her own
Systems Area.

Systems Areas provide data to their Reps to help make the
business decision (collaboration), and then sometimes take
the final decision and reverse or argue against at the management level.

There is little or no collaborative effort on the part of Systems
Mgrs to work together on these issues. They are instead used
to keeping competition and rivalrys going among themselves
and the Data Center Mgr.

The impact is a reduction or negating of technical needs and
a raising of political issues as a base for problem resolution
rather than technical expertise.

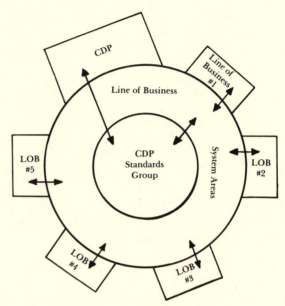

STDS Group and Systems Area Reps have achieved a substantial level of positive collaboration.

Each Rep has a degree of collaboration with own LOB Area. There is no collaboration effort among Systems Areas, and STDS person often has a split allegiance between STDS and own LOB (this dilutes level of collaborative effectiveness).

CDP communicates directly with STDS function (STDS is located within CDP ORG) and with each level on a one-on-one basis.

Five LOBs and CDP do not ordinarily work together on these issues.

As a result, the systems areas (one by one) began to complain about the poor job the standards area was doing, its failure to develop a proper standard or to revise or rescind the standard. Chaos was created as the systems needed special permission to run while "out of standard" and could not be scheduled automatically.

This situation continued until the customer complaints exceeded the data center performance levels and the standards manager was able to convince the data center manager of the problems with the no-card standard.

The standard was reissued in its original form and gradually order was restored.

Unfortunately, the standards group still feels the negative results of this situation. Users still point to this example when new standards to which they are opposed are recommended. Whenever a new standard is implemented, many people are still quick to ask if it will have as catastrophic results as the card standard.

CASE NO. 8: PERSONNEL ASSESSMENT CENTERS

The assessment of nonmanagerial, nonsupervisory employees by line and staff managers higher in the company hierarchy involves significant changes on the part of assessors. Managers assigned to the center for a "tour of duty" are selected from all areas of the business to provide a wide range of experience and background. Those selected are considered promotable, and have demonstrated competence in their previous assignments. All have functioned as a part of teams on various committees in the performance of their jobs, but not to the degree that the assessment process requires.

The nature of the assessment process requires three team members to make evaluations of six candidates over two days against 18 different variables judged to be predictable of supervisory ability.

The 18 variables are observed over two days while the candidates are involved in a number of interactive exercises. Independent reports are written by each assessor in preparation for joint rating and decision-making sessions about the candidates.

One assessor can't possibly observe all the behavioral

reactions of all six candidates, and must rely on the other team members to catch what he or she misses or misinterprets.

Unlike the normal work environment outside the assessment center sessions, assessors must develop an openness and trust early to ensure that candidates receive a complete and thorough evaluation. This need for a totally accurate evaluation promotes full disclosure and tests a manager's handling of sensitive information on candidates as well as self.

A support system quickly develops and allows managers to feel free to appear foolish because the evaluation task takes a higher priority. This situation is in direct contrast to committee work outside the center because one is often discussed by peers as being incompetent under the same circumstances.

Because of the interdependence necessary to function, the assessment task generates a cohesive team. Each assessor not performing his/her part affects the other two directly, and one person not completing the task clearly stands out. There is motivation to do your part as completely as possible. The success of the group demands cohesion for the entire team rather than individual efforts alone. Individual effort is recognized in high quality reports that make the overall task easier but don't affect the evaluative process.

The major factors that assessment managers face, which alter their behavior in the assessment process in contrast with line/staff managers, are as follows:

1. Empathy. An early concern for coassessors who have to feed the results back to candidates without glossing over any facts. Line and staff managers can and do evaluate poor performance in a general way that can leave the employee in doubt about his/her actual performance. The assessment process demands straightforward feedback to a candidate.

2. Conflict. It is easier to enter into heated debate over the type of behavior exhibited by a candidate because this ground rule has been clearly established. The input from any evaluator must come from written notes taken during the two days that the candidates were involved in the exercises at the assessment center. This is impossible in other operations of the organization because the acquisition of data comes from many sources and can be used in any manner.

3. Communication. The focus of the process dictates clarity of communication. Time is always taken to ensure that reports and readouts are clearly understood by each member of the team. Each assessor makes an effort to ask clarifying questions to test understanding, and doesn't make assumptions about what he or she thought a team member said. For a number of reasons, line and staff managers often let data go by and use their own view of the world to interpret what one or more of their peers intended to say.

4. Power and Influence. A forceful personality in an operational setting outside the center and within the normal operating practices of the organization can prove intimidating to a lot of people, but this is not helpful, nor is it utilized in the assessment process.

ANALYSIS OF CASES

Case numbers 2 and 3 provide clear examples of how change in structural components results in a more collaborative structure and a different organizational climate. It should be noted that this was not a drastic change in the notion of hierarchical authority, but it is clearly a step in that direction.

Case number 4 provides a clearer example of a subsystem that approached a collaborative way of functioning for a period of time. There were a variety of difficulties in this venture, and in some ways the outcome was predictable, given the context for the collaborative attempt.

Case numbers 5 and 8 provide additional descriptive support and demonstration of collaborative processes in organizational contexts. Both document the need for overriding task necessity and processes that may vary from task component to task component, but are, overall, consistent with the task outcomes expected by the remainder of the organization.

Case number 6 provides data to support the importance of a defined task and the impact that it can have, at least in the short run, on the process and outcome of the subsystem.

It is interesting that the chair is described as behaving in a dictatorial fashion even though the value system and the processes conform closely to the collaborative model. The chair was probably *very* emphatic about the tasks to be performed, and this is in keeping with the notion of functional differentiation.

It is also obvious that ultimate responsibility did not rest with the chair and this led to a keen sense of involvement on the part of the participants.

Case number 7 demonstrates the impact of a competitive (political is used in the case, although it is a clear case of competition for perceived scarce resources of power) process on the investment and task consequences of and for another subsystem within the organization. It exemplifies the impact that these processes can have on a subsystem attempting to apply a collaborative model without realizing the impact on these larger dynamics in the surrounding context on their own subsystem.

Subsystem Issues

These cases are consistent with attempts to function in a collaborative or participative fashion. Because functioning in this manner is extremely contrary to the usual ways of functioning, i.e., hierarchical structure and competition, there are tremendous difficulties inherent in any attempts to function in a collaborative and participative manner. As such, one encounters difficulties and pitfalls involved in functioning in a collaborative fashion.

First of all, it is vital that any system functioning in a collaborative fashion be extremely clear about the assumptions under which it is functioning. Those assumptions must be checked out very carefully, and implications for organizational *functioning* must be specified.

This becomes a particularly critical issue when the collaborative system attempts to interface with other social systems or organizations. Since most other systems are functioning in a hierarchical mode, they are not able to respond to a group or system that operates differently. There appears to be a need on the part of an outside system to put tremendous pressure on a collaborative system to function in a hierarchical and competitive way. Response to this pressure by members in a collaborative organization is manifested in nonproductive ways. Nonproductivity occurs when people behave in ways that they *assume* are consistent with an espoused value system, because they expect other people to be functioning in the same way. When a discrepancy emerges, individuals are likely to see and respond more quickly to a discrepancy between their own value system and behaviors. Since members within the collaborative organization have been part of the same socialization process as members of an outside organization, they still feel impacted by the reinforcement provided by the outside organization.

This reinforcement leads to a second concern/difficulty with regard to a collaborative organization. It is extremely critical that a collaborative organization implement a reward system that indeed meets the needs of its members, and reinforces collaborative, nonhierarchical, and noncompetitive behavior within that subsystem.

If this is not done, the likelihood of individual competing behaviors within the collaborative subsystem is extremely high. As individuals attempt to behave in ways that elicit rewards from both subsystems (the collaborative and the hierarchical), a rather neurotic or confused behavior will result. It will also confuse other members within the collaborative subsystem as to the motivation, commitment, and value system of individuals caught in this competing reward system structure.

A third critical area is the collaborative organization's value system as a social system, as well as the value system held by individual members. This value system must be explicit. It must also define behaviors that are appropriate for a collaborative value system. If not, motives and values counter to the collaborative organization will be ascribed to members.

The differences between a collaborative organization functioning with clear lines of authority and one functioning with a focus on a functional division of labor with clearly differentiated functions must be specified. A collaborative organization faces the same difficulties with which a hierarchical organization struggles. Often what starts out to be a differentiation of function turns into not only a differentiated function but differentiated authority as well. This differentiated authority is counter to the basic notion of a collaboratively functioning system. Differential skill levels among members of the organization present great difficulties in this type of organizational structure. It is extremely important that differential skill levels — if they exist — be identified. In terms of behavior, the implications for these differential skill levels need to be identified.

One of the greatest concerns emerging in any organization attempting to function in a different way from the main-stream of organizations (outside the major accepted value systems and behaviors) is the discrepancy that occurs between value systems and attitudes and behavior.

In any organization the discrepancy between espoused values and the concurrent behaviors makes it difficult for other members to function. Organizational members respond primarily to the behaviors of other members, rather than to the espoused value system of those individuals. Because of the way people respond in organizations, it is necessary for a collaborative organization to specify the behaviors that are expected from members within that organization.

These cases should give the current manager some ideas of how to attain a collaborative process or structure. It should also be noted that these new systems do not run automatically! They need continual monitoring and assessment to function successfully. Managers must realize that the subsystem goals and processes may be incompatible with the larger system, and that their job may well entail the management of these interfaces.

The cases have illustrated the importance of both the conceived cultural values and the operative organizational philosophies in initiating and maintaining a collaborative model in an organizational context.

The cases also exemplify functional dispersal, nonelevated roles, linked objectives, and functional interdependence, as well as pluralism, planning as a process, and the importance of interdependence.

Chapter 10

THE FUTURE:
AN UNCERTAIN REALITY

At what appears to be a stopping point for this effort, I am suddenly struck by the impossibility of affecting a revolutionary change in organizational life. I have already identified some of the difficulties of applying a collaborative model to a hierarchical organization. It seems an overwhelming task and, at the same time, an exciting challenge.

I presented data that describes how organizations function and then presented some alternatives for organizational functioning in the future.

I alternate between being wildly optimistic about the possibilities and being doggedly pessimistic about the probabilities. There are a variety of sources of that optimism, not the least of which is some of the reported (predicted) trends impacting the future of organizational life.

The Corporate Responsibility Planning Service (1976) has identified ten shifts in the relationships between employers and employees. Several of these are directly related to the issues involved in the movement of organizations from a hierarchical to a collaborative orientation.

These shifts are also consistent with the conceived cultural values and the operative organizational philosophies identified in Chapters 5 and 6.

Shift 1:   Job Fit
Employers will have to make a much greater effort to ensure the optimum match of employees and jobs.
Shift 2:   Personal Development
Recognizing a generally greater value placed by employees on personal growth and expansion, employers will have to provide comprehensive, ongoing management and organizational development activities, not all of which will be limited to job-related skills.
Shift 3:   Nonfinancial Compensation
While direct financial compensation will probably never be completely supplanted, there will be less emphasis placed on it, especially as personal income taxes rise.
Shift 4:   Decreasing Importance of Academic Credentials
While the overall value of academic attainment will remain high, the degree to which employees are required to have academic credentials to qualify for positions will be reduced.
Shift 5:   Employee Involvement in Decision Making
Employees at all levels will have a greater role in decision making and overall governance.
Shift 6:   Employee Counseling
Prominent among the shifts away from the traditional approach to human resource management, is the trend toward greater corporate involvement with the personal lives of employees and their problems.
Shift 7:   Input to Job Transfers and Assignments
Increasingly, employees will have the right to refuse transfers and job assignments without negatively affecting their career standing.
Shift 8.:   Blurred Job Distinctions
As the national workforce becomes increasingly service oriented (education, government, insurance, leisure, banking, retail,

etc.), the distinction between white and blue collar, and professional and nonprofessional will blur.

Shift 9.:   Employee Rights

The Constitution's Bill of Rights, the protection of which citizens enjoy, will become a source of protection for employees.

Shift 10:   Employee Ownership

Employee ownership of corporations through pension funds and stock ownership will increase. (pp. 2–6).

Several of these shifts are directly related to collaborative organizational values, structures, and processes. The trends in job fit, personal development, employee involvement in decision making, transfers, job distinctions, and employee ownership are particularly central. The others are also consistent with a collaborative framework for organizational functioning.

Major corporations that are or have engaged in rather radical attempts at organizational restructuring and adoption of alternative organizational processes have already been identified and are just cause for optimism.

In addition, several European countries including West Germany, Yugoslavia, Sweden, Great Britain, and Norway are continuing to report efforts at legislation to support worker ownership and influence over the organization.

Employee values are changing as well, according to a recent study reported by Cooper, Morgan, Foley, and Kaplan (1979). This study reports survey data over a 25-year period that implies there is an emerging *hierarchy gap* in organizations. That is, there are obvious differences between managers and clerical and hourly workers, with the managers usually being the more satisfied.

In addition to these findings, several others have emerged from the survey data. They are:

1.   Employees agree that their company is not as good a place to work as it once was. Managers' perceptions of improvements have steadily decreased over 17 years.

2. Hourly and clerical employees express a great deal of growing discontent.
3. Pay is rated favorably but does not offset the feeling that employees are not respected as individuals in the organizations.
4. There is a downward trend in feelings of equity, and expectations for advancement are the lowest ever.
5. Employees expect employers to do something about their problems, but they do not believe companies are responding.

Cooper, et al. summarize the implications of these findings for management and organizations in their concluding paragraph with the following:

> What is undeniably required, however, is that corporations recognize the new realities within which they must function. The crucial issues then become the degree to which management can successfully identify, anticipate, and address these changing values as they surface, or before they surface, in their own organization. But, make no mistake about it, changing employee values are no myth. They will be realities that companies must face in the 1980s. (p. 125)

Articles appearing in newspapers are more frequently dealing with issues related to hope and the need for organizations to consider alternative organizational frameworks and perspectives. *The Wall Street Journal, The New York Times,* and *The Hartford Courant* have all carried articles on issues and dynamics related to the need for major changes predicted for the future — all having a huge impact on life in organizations.

These articles discuss the predicted reduction of promotional opportunities at all levels in the organization (Drucker, 1970); they speculate on the possibilities and implications for the industrial democracy experimentation in Germany for and in organizations in this country (Furlong, 1979); they report conferences attended by firms whose managements wish to improve the quality of working life (Smith, R., 1979); and they discuss a professor's continued attempts to formulate and develop the United States Academy of Peace and Conflict Resolution (UPI, 1979).

A lofty goal indeed! Yet in harmony with the broader implications and ramifications of collaborative structures and processes.

A vice-president of a large insurance company, in personal correspondence, also raised several issues that bear on the future of organizational contexts. First, if affirmative action remains a potent force in organizational hiring, it may well result in more women and third-world peoples being eligible for promotions in organizations. Alternative forms of organizational functioning seem necessary to reduce the effects of competition and move toward an atmosphere of cooperation in organizations. If this is not the case, environments will likely become very tense and erupt in powerful competitively based struggles for dominance of organizational resources.

Second, if there is a decrease in opportunities for meaningful promotions, unionism may emerge as protection for the attainment of some control in the workplace. Unless something changes radically, and unions start to bargain for increased quality of working life, a tremendous struggle for perceived (and perhaps actual) resources will result. It does not appear that unions, as presently oriented (although the orientation may still be appropriate for many present circumstances), will provide viable strategies and methodologies to alter drastically the structures and processes in organizations. The unions and management are basically in an adversary position. Very often that leads to a rearrangement of the status quo, but not to a basic alteration in the structures and processes influencing the distribution of power. Ultimately this power distribution must shift if organizations are to be altered in the future.

Without this basic shift, some improvement in the nature of life in organizations may be anticipated; however, this will only amount to a cosmetic approach that will wear away and need continued reapplication in the form of new programs.

If the authority structure and the power distribution are not altered, and further, if competitive hierarchical arrangements are not eliminated, one can look forward to the continued emergence of technology to increase efficiency in organizations, while making the work itself more boring and tedious.

If efficiency experts do not factor in growth potentials for individuals, if they do not change the basic assumptions around which organizations are built and maintained, programs dealing with the outflow of personal resentment from this kind of treatment can only increase. Current assumptions that influence job design will have to change drastically if organizational structure and process are to change.

It is hard to imagine what organizations would be like if power were really shared — if employees really had control over their lives in organizations. They hardly have the vocabulary to discuss, let alone conceive, what these organizations would be like. It is easy to get in touch with the feelings that would emerge in those organizations; yet there is a great deal of fear attached to this speculation.

At least, many people know how to survive elegantly in organizations as they presently operate, and most individuals have developed skills to beat the system at its own game, or make it look like they are conforming while trying to remain free in their "real" attitudes and feelings.

Many individuals may have even tried to behave in collaborative ways, but quickly "matured" when they learned that those ways were incongruent with the "rigors of organizational life."

"It's a tough world out there," they've been told , and "you have to play tough to survive." Naturally, survival is important to all.

Personal identity is often tied closely with work. People know who they are by what they do. At the very least, they behave as if their work lets others know who they are. Titles give confidence, and promotions give status — even if at the expense of others.

It is a circular process and it perpetuates the status quo. There may be hope, but only if the control mechanisms, the "things" that "press the buttons," can be recognized.

The model, framework, and issues exposed in this work are in no way resolved — partly because of the nature of the model itself.

I have attempted to pull together some of the support that I see for these new organizational forms, and I have attempted to present some perspectives about this "new" type of organization. While I may have taken some drastic steps in this regard, it must be remembered that the journey is just beginning, and there is a long way to go.

BIBLIOGRAPHY

Ackoff, R. L. *Redesigning the future: A systems approach to societal planning.* New York: John Wiley & Sons, 1974.

Aiken, M., & Hage, J. Organizational interdependence and intra-organizational structure. *American Sociological Review,* 1968, *63,* pp. 912-930.

Alexander, K. O. Issues in job enlargement, job enrichment, worker participation and shared authority. *American Journal of Economics & Sociology,* Jan. 1975, *34,* pp. 43-54.

Alinsky, S. D. *Rules for radicals.* New York: Random House, 1972.

Almack, J. C. Mental efficiency of consulting pairs. *Educational Research Bulletin,* 1930, *9,* pp. 2-3.

Anderson, H. H. Domination and integration in the social behavior of kindergarten children in an experimental play situation. *Genetic Psychology Monographs,* 1939, *2,* pp. 357-385.

Appley, D. G. The changing place of work for women and men. *Beyond sex role stereotypes,* Alice Sargent, Ed. West Publishing Co., 1976.

Aram, J. D., Cyril, P. M. & Esbeck, E. S. Relationship of collaborative interpersonal relationships to individual satisfaction and organizational performance. *Administrative Science Quarterly,* Sept. 1971, *76* (*3*), pp. 289-296.

Argyris, C. *Interpersonal competence and organizational effectiveness.* Homewood, Ill.: Dorsey Press, 1962.

Argyris, C. The incompleteness of social psychological theory. *American Psychology,* October 1969, *24,* pp. 893-908.

Argyris, C. *Intervention theory and method.* Reading, Mass.: Addison-Wesley, 1970.

Argyris, C. *The applicability of organizational sociology.* Cambridge: Cambridge University Press, 1972.

Argyris, C. Dangers in applying results from experimental social psychology. *American Psychologist,* April 1975, *30* (*4*), pp. 469-485.

Argyris, C., & Schon, D. *Organizational learning: A theory of action perspective.* Reading, Mass.: Addison-Wesley, 1978.

Aristotle. *The politics,* Translated by T. A. Sinclair. Baltimore: Penguin Books, 1962.

Asch, S. E. *Social psychology.* Englewood Cliffs, N. J.: Prentice-Hall, 1952.

Aubert, W. Competition and dissensus: Two types of conflict and conflict resolution. *Journal of Conflict Resolution,* Vol. 7, March 1963, pp. 41-42.

Back, K. W. Influence through social communication. *Journal of Abnormal and Social Psychology,* 1951, *46,* pp. 9-23.

Baker, E. H. A pre-Civil War simulation for teaching American history. In S. S. Boocock & E. O. Schild, Eds., *Simulation games in learning.* Beverly Hills, Calif.: Sage Publications, 1968.

Barnard, C. Functions and pathology of status systems in formal organizations, William I. White, Ed., *Industry and society.* New York: McGraw-Hill, 1946.

Bass, B. M. The production organization exercise. In W. W. Cooper, H. J. Leavitt, & M. W. Shelley, Eds., *New perspectives in organization research.* New York: John Wiley & Sons, 1964.

Bavelas, A. Leadership: Man and function. *Administrative Science Quarterly,* March 1960, *4,* pp. 491-498.

Beckhard, R. *Organization development: Strategies and models.* Reading, Mass.: Addison-Wesley, 1969.

Bennis, W. G. Organizational developments and the fate of bureaucracy. Invited address, Division of Industrial and Business Psychology, American Psychological Association, Sept. 5, 1964, pp. 6-7.

Bennis, W. G. Changing Organizations. *Journal of Applied Behavioral Science,* 1966a, *2 (3),* pp. 247-263.

Bennis, W. G. *Beyond bureaucracy: Essays on the development and evolution of human organization.* New York: McGraw-Hill, 1966b.

Berkowitz, L. Effects of perceived dependency relationships upon conformity to group expectations. *Journal of Abnormal and Social Psychology,* 1957, *55,* pp. 50-54.

Bierstedt, R. An analysis of social power. *American Sociological Review,* 1950, *15,* p. 730.

Blake, R., & Mouton, J. Reactions to intergroup competition under win-lose conditions. *Management Science,* July 1961, *4 (4),* pp. 420-435.

Blanchard, F. A., Adelman, L., & Cook, S. W. The effect of group success and failure upon interpersonal attraction in cooperating interracial groups. *Journal of Personality and Social Psychology.* 1974

Blau, P. M. *The dynamics of bureaucracy.* Chicago: University of Chicago Press, 1963.

Blau, P. M. *Exchange and power in social life.* New York: John Wiley & Sons, Inc., 1964.

Blau, P. M. & Scott, W. R. Formal Organizations. A comparative Approach. Scranton: Chandler Publishing Co., 1962.

Blauner, R. *Alienation and freedom.* Chicago: University of Chicago Press, 1964.

Bodin, J. *Method for the easy comprehension of history.* Translated by
Beatrice Reynolds. New York: Columbia University Press, 1945.

Bogart, D. H., & Tipps, H. C. The Threat from Species O. *The futurist,*
April 1973.

Bonoma, T. V., Tedeschi, J. T., & Helm, B. Some effects of target cooperation and reciprocated promises on conflict resolution. *Sociometry,*
1974, *37,* pp. 251-261.

Boslooper, T., & Hayes, M. *The femininity game.* New York: Stein & Day,
1973.

Bryant, B. K., Crockenberg, S. B., & Wilce, L. S. *The educational context
for the study of cooperation and helpful concern for others.* Paper
presented at the convention of the American Educational Research
Association, Chicago, April 1974.

Burns, T., & Stalker, G. M. *The management of innovation.* London:
Tavistock Publications, 1961.

Carew, D. K. Some necessary values: Toward collaborative organizations.
Unpublished paper, University of Massachusetts, 1976.

Cartwright, D. Influence, leadership, control. *Handbook of organizations.* J. G. March, Ed. Chicago: Rand McNally, 1965.

Chapin, I. S. Social institutions and voluntary associations. In J. B.
Gittler, Ed. *Review of sociology: Analysis of a decade.* New York:
John Wiley & Sons, 1957, p. 273.

Chapman, J. R., & Feder, R. B. The effect of external incentives on
improvement. *Journal of Educational Psychology,* 1917, *8,* pp.
469-474.

Chavoor, S., & Davidson, B. *The 50– meter jungle: How Olympic gold
medal swimmers are made.* New York: Coward, McCann, & Geogh-
egan, Inc., 1973.

Chandler, A. *Strategy and structure.* Garden City, N.Y.: Anchor Books,
1966.

Claru, A. W., Ed. *Experimenting with organizational life: The action
research approach.* New York: Plenum Press, 1976.

Clayton, D. Competition motivates typewriting students. *The Balance
Sheet,* December 1964, *46 (4).*

Clifford, M. M. Motivational effects of competition and goal-setting in
reward and nonreward conditions. *Journal of Experimental Education,* 1971, *39,* pp. 11-16.

Collins, R. *Conflict sociology: Toward an explanatory science.* New
York: Academic Press, Inc., 1975. (Includes 32 testable causal princi-
ples/hypotheses re: competition in America, pp. 216-219.)

Connally, J. B. A time for toughness in America. *Reader's Digest,* Oct.
1972.

Cook, S. W. Motives in a conceptual analysis of attitude-related behavior. In W. J. Arnold & D. Levine, Eds., *Nebraska symposium on motivation*. Lincoln, Nebraska: University of Nebraska Press, 1969, pp. 179-231.

Cooper, M. R., Morgan, B. S., Foley, P. M. & Kaplan, L. B. Changing employee values: Deepening discontent? *Harvard Business Review*, 1979, *57 (1)*, pp. 117-125.

Corporate Responsibility Planning Service. *Ten shifts in the employee/employer relationship*. Philadelphia: Human Resources Network, 1976.

Coser, L. *The functions of social conflict*. New York: The Free Press, 1956.

Crockenberg, S., & Bryant, B. *Helping and sharing behavior in cooperative and competitive classrooms*. Paper presented at the meetings of the Society on Research in Child Development, Philadelphia, March 1973.

Crombag, H. R. Cooperation and competition in means-independent triads: A replication. *Journal of Personality and Social Psychology*, 1966, *4*, pp. 692-695.

Culbert, S. A. *The organization trap and how to get out of it*. New York: Basic Books, Inc., 1974.

Dachler, H. P., & Wilpert, B. Conceptual dimensions and boundaries of participation in organizations: A critical evaluation. *Administrative Science Quarterly*, March 1978, *23*, pp. 1-39.

Dahl, R. *After the revolution? Authority in a good society*. New Haven, Conn.: Yale University Press, 1970.

Dalton, G. W. Diagnosing interdepartmental conflict. *Harvard Business Review*, Sept.-Oct. 1963, pp. 121-132.

Darwin, C. *The descent of man*. New York: Appleton, 1880.

Darwin, F. *The life and letters of Charles Darwin*. New York: Appleton, 1887.

Davis, K., & Moore, W. E. Some principles of stratification. *American Sociological Review*, April 1945, *10*, pp. 242-249.

Deutsch, M. "A theory of cooperation and competition." *Human Relations*, 1949a, *2*, pp. 129-151.

Deutsch, M. *An experimental study of the effects of cooperation and competition in group success*. Human Relations, 1949b, *2*, pp. 199-231.

Deutsch, M. Trust and suspicion. *Journal of Conflict Resolution*, 1958, *2*, pp. 265-279.

Deutsch, M. Some factors affecting membership, motivation and achievement motivation. *Human Relations*, 1959, *12*, pp. 81-85.

Deutsch, M. The effects of cooperation and competition upon group process. In D. Cartwright & A. Zander, Eds., *Group dynamics* (2nd ed.). New York: Harper & Row, 1960, pp. 414-448.

Deutsch, M. Cooperation and trust: Some theoretical notes. In M. R. Jones, Ed., *Nebraska symposium on motivation.* Lincoln, Neb.: University of Nebraska Press, 1962, pp. 275-320.

Deutsch, M. Productive and destructive conflict. *Journal of Social Issues,* 1969a, *25 (1)*, pp. 7-42.

Deutsch, M. Socially relevant science: Reflections on some studies of interpresonal conflict. *American Psychologist,* 1969b, *24,* pp. 1076-1092.

Deutsch, M. *The resolution of conflict.* New Haven: Yale University Press, 1973.

Deutsch, M., & Krauss, R. Studies of interpersonal bargaining. *Journal of Conflict Resolution,* 1962, *6,* pp. 52-76.

DeVries, D., & Mescon, I. *Using TGT and the Moses De Witt Elementary School: A preliminary report.* Mimeographed report, Center for Social Organization of Schools, Johns Hopkins University, 1974.

DeVries, D. L. & Edwards, K. J. Learning games and student teams: their effects on classroom process. *American Educational Research Journal,* 1973, *10,* pp. 307-318.

DeVries, D. L. & Edwards, K. J. Cooperation in the classroom: toward a theory of alternative reward-task classroom structures. Paper presented at the annual meeting of the American Educational Research Association, Chicago, April, 1974.

DeVries, D. L., Edwards, K. J., & Wells, E. H. Teams-games-tournament in the social studies classroom: Effects on academic achievement, student attitudes, cognitive beliefs, and classroom climate. Report #173, Center for Social Organization of Schools, Johns Hopkins University, 1974.

Down, A. *Inside bureaucracy.* Waltham, Mass.: Little, Brown & Co., 1968.

Drucker, P. Baby-boom problems. *The Wall Street Journal,* February 5, 1979.

Dubin, R., Ed. *Handbook of work organization and society.* Chicago: Rand McNally, 1976.

Duncan, R. B. Characteristics of organizational environments and perceived uncertainty. *Administrative Science Quarterly,* September 1972, *17 (3),* pp. 313-327.

Dunn, R. E., & Goldman, M. Competition and noncompetition in relationship to satisfaction and feelings toward own group and non-group members. *Journal of Social Psychology,* 1966, *68,* pp. 299-311.

Dunnette, M. D., Ed. *Handbook of industrial and organizational psychology.* Chicago: Rand McNally, 1976.

Dutton, J. M., & Walton, R. E. Interdepartmental conflict and cooperation: Two contrasting studies. In J. W. Lorsch & P. R. Lawrence, *Managing group and intergroup relations.* Homewood, Ill.: Richard D. Irwin, 1972, pp. 285-304.

Edwards, W. Behavioral decision theory. In W. Edwards, Ed., *Decision making.* Baltimore: Penguin Books, 1967, pp. 65-95.

Eiseman, J. W. A third-party consultation model for resolving recurring conflicts collaboratively. *Journal of Applied Behavioral Science,* special issue: Collaboration in work settings. Edited by D. Appley; A. E. Winder; D. K. Carew; J. W. Eiseman; F. E. Finch; & W. A. Kraus. 1977, *13* (*3*) pp. 303-314.

Ellul, J. *The technological society.* New York: Vintage Books, 1964.

Emerson, R. M. Power-dependence relations. *American Sociological Review,* 1962, *27,* pp. 31-40.

Emery & Trist. *Towards a social ecology.* New York: Plenum Press, 1973.

Etzioni, A., Ed. *Complex organizations: A sociological reader.* New York: Holt, Rinehart & Winston, 1961.

Evan, W. Toward a theory of interorganizational relations. *Management Science,* 1965, *11,* pp. B217-B230.

Ewing, D. W. *Freedom inside the organization: Bringing civil liberties to the workplace.* New York: McGraw-Hill, 1977.

Fallding, H. Functional analysis in sociology. *American Sociological Review,* 1963, *28* (*1*), pp. 5-13.

Fay, A. S. *The effects of cooperation and competition on learning and recall.* Unpublished master's thesis, George Peabody College, 1970.

Ferguson, C. K., & Kelley, H. H. Significant factors in overevaluation of own-group's product. *Journal of Abnormal and Social Psychology,* 1964, *69,* pp. 223-228.

Festinger, L. A. *A theory of cognitive dissonance.* Evanston, Ill.: Row Peterson, 1957.

Filley, A. C., & House, R. J. *Managerial process and organizational behavior.* Glenview, Ill.: Scott, Foresman & Co., 1969.

Filley, A. C. *Interpersonal conflict resolution.* Glenview: Ill.: Scott, Foresman & Co., 1975.

Finch, F. E. Collaborative leadership in work settings. *Journal of Applied Behavioral Science,* special issue: Collaboration in work settings. Edited by D. G. Appley, A. E. Winder, D. K. Carew, J. W. Eiseman, F. E. Finch, & W. A. Kraus. 1977, *13* (*3*), pp. 292-302.

Fisch, G. G. Line-staff is obsolete. *The Harvard Business Review,* Sept.-Oct. 1961, pp. 67-79.

Forrester, J. W. A new corporate design. *Industrial Management Review*, July, 1965.

Fouraker, L., & Stopford, J. M. Organizational structure and the multinational strategy. *Administrative Science Quarterly*, June 1968, *13*, pp. 47-64.

Freire, P. *Pedagogy of the oppressed*. New York: Herder and Herder, 1971.

Freire, P. *Education for critical consciousness*. New York: The Seabury Press, 1973.

French, J. R. P. Group productivity. In H. Guetzkow, Ed., *Groups, leadership and men*. Pittsburgh: Carnegie Press, 1951, pp. 44-55.

French, J. R. P., & Raven, B. The bases of social power. In *Studies in social power*, D. Cartwright, Ed. University of Michigan, 1959.

Fromm, E. *To have or to be?* New York: Harper & Row, 1976.

Fuller, R. B. *Operating manual for spaceship earth*. New York: Simon & Schuster, 1969.

Furlong, J. Workers in the board room. *The Wall Street Journal*, March 12, 1979.

Galbraith, J. R. *Designing complex organizations*. Reading, Mass.: Addison-Wesley, 1973.

Galbraith, J. R. *Organization design*. Reading, Mass.: Addison-Wesley, 1977.

Gardner, J. *Self-renewal: The individual and the innovative society*. New York: Harper Calophon Books, 1965.

Gerard, H. B. The effects of different dimensions of disagreement on the communication process in small groups. *Human Relations*, 1953, 7, pp. 13-25.

Gillman, G. An inquiry into the nature and use of authority. In Mason Haire, Ed., *Organization theory in industrial practice*. New York: John Wiley & Sons, 1962.

Glidewell, J. C. *Choice points: Essays on the emotional problems of living with people*. Cambridge: M.I.T. Press, 1970.

Golembiewski, R. T., & Blumberg, A., Eds. *Sensitivity training and the laboratory approach: Reading about concepts and applications*. Itasca, Ill.: F. E. Peacock Publishers, Inc., 1970.

Gorney, R. *The human agenda*. New York: Bantam Books, 1973.

Gottheil, E. Changes in social perceptions contingent upon competing or cooperating. *Sociometry*, 1955, *18*, pp. 132-137.

Greenberg, E. S. Consequences of worker participation: A clarification of the theoretical literature. *Social Science Quarterly*, Sept. 1975, *56*, pp. 191-209.

Greene, G. *The human factor*. New York: Avon Books, 1978.

Greenfield, T. B. Organizations as social inventions: Rethinking assumptions about change. *Journal of Applied Behavioral Science*, 1973, *9* (5) pp. 551-573.

Grossack, M. M. Some effects of competition upon small group behavior. *Journal of Abnormal and Social Psychology*, 1954, *49*, pp. 341-348.

Guetzkow, H., & Gyr, J. An analysis of conflict in decision-making groups. *Human Relations*, 1954, *7*, pp. 367-382.

Guetzkow, H. Relations among organizations. In R. Bowers, Ed., *Studies on behavior in organizations*. Athens, Georgia: University of Georgia Press, 1966, pp. 13-44.

Gurdjieff, G. *The herald of coming good: First appeal to contemporary humanity*. New York: Samuel Weiser, Inc., 1974.

Gurnee, H. Learning under competitive and collaborative sets. *Journal of Experimental Social Psychology*, 1968, *4*, pp. 26-34.

Haddad, C. J. *Worker participation: Industrial democracy, or corporate manipulation*. Unpublished paper, Labor Relations and Research Center, University of Massachusetts, December, 1975.

Hage, J., & Aiken, M. Routine technology, social structure and organizational goals. *Administrative Science Quarterly*, 1969, *14*, pp. 366-377.

Haines, D. B., & McKeachie, W. J. Cooperative versus competitive discussion methods in teaching introductory psychology. *Journal of Educational Psychology*, 1967, *58*, pp. 386-390.

Hall, R. H. Intraorganizational structure variation. *Administrative Science Quarterly*, December 1962, 7 (*3*), pp. 295-308.

Hammond, B. Participation: How to make it work. *Vision*, December 1974, pp. 43-47.

Hammond, L. K., & Goldman, M. Competition and noncompetition and its relationship to individual and group productivity. *Sociometry*, 1961, *24*, pp. 46-60.

Hampton, D. R., Summer, C. E., & Webber, R. A. *Organizational behavior and the practice of management*. Glenview: Scott, Foresman, & Co., 1973.

Harlow, D., & Hanke, J. J. *Behavior in organizations: Text, readings, and cases*. Boston: Little, Brown & Company, 1975.

Heider, F. *The psychology of interpersonal relations*. New York: John Wiley & Sons, 1958.

Hellriegel, D., & Slocum, J. W. *Management: A contingency approach*. Addison-Wesley, 1974.

Hellriegel, D. *Organizational behavior: Contingency views*. New York: West Publishing Co., 1976.

Herbert, T. T. *Dimensions of organizational behavior*. New York: Macmillan, 1976.

Herbst, P. *Socio-technical design: Strategies in multidisciplinary research*. New York: Harper & Row, Inc., and London: Tavistock Publications, 1974.

Herrick, N. Q. *The quality of work and its outcomes: Estimating increases in labor productivity.* Columbus, Ohio: The Academy for Contemporary Problems, 1975.

Herrick, N. Q., & Maccoby, M. *Humanizing work: A priority goal of the 1970s.* Hearings before the Subcommittee on Labor and Public Welfare, 1972.

Hersey, P., & Blanchard, K. H. *Management of organizational behavior* (3rd ed.). Englewood Cliffs, N.J.: Prentice-Hall, 1977.

Herzberg, F. *Work and the nature of man.* Cleveland: World Publishing Co., 1966.

Hinrichs, J. R. Measurement of reasons for resignation of professionals: Questionnaire vs. co. and consultant exit interviews. *Journal of Applied Psychology,* Aug. 1975, *60,* pp. 530-532.

Hobbes, T. *Leviathan.* New York: Macmillan, 1947.

Hobbes, T. *The citizen.* New York: Appleton-Century-Crofts, 1949.

Hume, D. *Essays: Moral, political, and literary.* Edited by T. H. Green & T. H. Grose. London: Longmans, Green, 1, 1907.

Hummel, R. *The bureaucratic experience.* New York: St. Martin's Press, 1977.

Hurlock, E. B. Use of group rivalry as an incentive. *Journal of Abnormal and Social Psychology,* 1927, *22,* pp. 278-290.

Husband, R. W. Cooperation versus solitary problem solving. *Journal of Social Psychology,* 1940, *11,* pp. 405-409.

Ilgen, D. R., & O'Brien, G. *The effects of task organization and member compatibility on leader-member relations in small groups.* Urbana: University of Illinois, 1968.

Ingalls, J. D. *Human energy: The critical factor for individuals and organizations.* Reading, Mass.: Addison-Wesley, 1976.

Johnson, D. W. Role reversal: A summary and review of the research. *International Journal of Group Tensions,* 1971, *1,* pp. 318-334.

Johnson, D. W. *Student attitudes toward cooperation and competition in a midwestern school district.* Unpublished report, University of Minnesota, 1973.

Johnson, D. W. Cooperativeness and social perspective taking. *Journal of Personality and Social Psychology,* 1974a.

Johnson, D. W. *Affective perspective taking and cooperative predisposition.* Mimeographed report, University of Minnesota. Submitted for publication, 1974b.

Johnson, D. W., & Lewicki, R. J. The initiation of superordinate goals. *Journal of Applied Behavioral Science,* 1969, *5,* pp. 9-24.

Johnson, D. W., & Johnson, R. T. *Learning together and alone: Cooperation, competition, and individualization.* Englewood Cliffs: Prentice-Hall, Inc., 1975.

Johnson, R. T. Cooperation in the elementary science classroom: Perception and preferences of sixth grade students. University of Minnesota, Mimeographed report, 1972.

Johnson, R. T., Johnson, D. W., & Bryant, B. Cooperation and competition in the classroom: Perceptions and preferences as related to students' feelings of personal control. *Elementary School Journal*, 1973, *73*, pp. 306-313.

Jones, S. C., & Vroom, V. H. Division of labor and performance under cooperative and competitive conditions. *Journal of Abnormal and Social Psychology*, 1964, *68*, pp. 313-320.

Julian, J. W., & Perry, F. A. Cooperation contrasted with intra-group and inter-group competition. *Sociometry*, 1967, *30*, pp. 79-90.

Kagan, S., & Madsen, M. C. Cooperation and competition of Mexican-American and Anglo-American children of two ages under four instructional sets. *Developmental Psychology*, 1971, *5*, pp. 32-39.

Kagan, S. & Madsen, M. C. Rivalry in Anglo-American and Mexican children of two ages. *Journal of Personality and Social Psychology*, 1972, *24*, pp. 214-220.

Kanter, R. M. *Commitment and Community*. Cambridge: Harvard University Press, 1972.

Kanter, R. M. *Men and women of the corporation*. New York: Basic Books, Inc., 1977.

Katz, D., & Georgopoulos, B. Organizations in a changing world. *Journal of Applied Behavioral Science*, 1971, 7 (*3*), pp. 342-370.

Kefauver, E. *In a few hands: Monopoly power in America*. New York: Pantheon Books, Inc., 1965.

Kelly, H. H., & Stahelski, A. J. Social interaction basis of cooperators' and competitors' beliefs about others. *Journal of Personality and Social Psychology*, 1970, *16*, pp. 66-91.

Kelly, H. H., & Thibaut, J. W. Group problem solving. In G. Lindzey & E. Aronson, Eds., *The handbook of social psychology* (2nd ed., Vol. 4). Reading, Mass: Addison-Wesley, 1969.

Khaldun, I. *An Arab philosophy of history*. Translated by C. Issawi. London: John Murray, 1950.

Kingdom, D. R. *Matrix organization*. New York: Harper & Row, 1973.

Klein, J. *The study of groups*. London: Routledge, 1956.

Kogan, N., & Wallach, M. A. Risk taking as a function of the situation, the person, and the group. In G. Mandler, P. Mussen, N. Kogan, & M. A. Wallach, *New directions in psychology*, (Vol. 3), pp. 224-266. New York: Holt, Rinehart & Winston, 1967.

Kohn, M. L. Occupational structure and alienation. *American Journal of Sociology*, 1976, *82*, pp. 111-129.

Kolb, D. A., Rubin, I. M., & McIntyre, J. M. *Organizational psychology: An experiential approach.* Englewood Cliffs: Prentice-Hall, Inc., 1974.

Kraus, W. A., Appley, D. G., & Carew, D. C. Development of an applied behavioral science alliance. In W. W. Burke, Ed., *Current issues and strategies in organizational development.* New York: Human Sciences Press, 1977, pp. 285-304.

Krauss, R. M., & Deutsch, M. Communication in interpersonal bargaining. *Journal of Personality and Social Psychology,* 1966, *4,* pp. 572-577.

Krugman, S. F. Cooperation versus individual efficiency in problem solving. *Journal of Educational Psychology,* 1944, *35,* pp. 91-100.

Laing, R. D. *Knots.* New York: Vintage Books, 1970.

Laughlin, P. R., & McGlynn, R. P. Cooperative versus competitive concept attainment as a function of sex and stimulus display. *Journal of Social Psychology,* 1967, *7,* pp. 498-501.

Laumann, E. O., Siegel, P. M., & Hodge, R. W., Eds. *The logic of social hierarchies.* Chicago: Markham, 1970.

Lawrence, P., & Lorsch, J. *Organization and environment.* Division of Research, Graduate School of Business Administration, Harvard University, 1967.

Leavitt, H. J., Dill, W. R., & Eyring, H. B. *The organizational world.* New York: Harcourt Brace Jovanovich, Inc., 1973.

Leavitt, H. Collaborative models: Influence without power. *Managerial psychology* (third ed.). Chicago: The University of Chicago Press, 1972, pp. 158-169.

Levine, S., & White, P. Exchange as a conceptual framework for the study of interorganizational relationships. *Administrative Science Quarterly,* 1961, *5,* pp. 583-601.

Levy, S. *Experimental study of group norms: The effects of group cohesiveness upon social conformity.* Ph.D. dissertation, New York University, 1953.

Lewin, K. Group decision and social change. In E. E. Maccoby, T. N. Newcomb, & E. L. Hartley, Eds., *Readings in social psychology.* New York: Holt, Rinehart & Winston, 1958.

Likert, R. *New patterns in management.* New York: McGraw-Hill, 1961.

Lippitt, G. L. *Organization renewal: Achieving viability in a changing world.* New York: Appleton-Century-Crofts, 1969.

Lippitt, G. L. Quality of work life: Organization renewal in action. *Training and Developing Journal,* July 1978, *32,* pp. 4-10.

Lischerow, J. A., & Wall, T. D. Employee participation: An experimental field study. *Human Relations,* Dec. 1975, *28,* pp. 863-884.

Litterer, J. A. *The analysis of organizations* (2nd ed.). New York: John Wiley & Sons, Inc., 1973.

Locke, E. A. Toward a theory of task motivation and incentives. *Organizational Behavior and Human Performance*, 1968, *3*, pp. 179-180.

Locke, E. A. Toward a theory of task motivation and incentives. *Organizational Behavior and Human Performance*, 1968, *3*, pp. 179-180. In A. J. Melcher, *Structure and process of organizations: A systems approach.* Englewood Cliffs: Prentice-Hall, Inc., 1976.

Lorsch, J. W., & Lawrence, P. R. Organizing for product innovation. *Harvard Business Review*, Jan.–Feb. 1965. In D. R. Hampton, C. E. Summer, & R. A. Webber, *Organizational behavior and the practice of management.* Glenview, Ill.: Scott, Foresman, & Co., 1973.

Lowi, T. J. *The end of liberalism: Ideology, policy, and the crisis of public authority.* New York: W. W. Norton, 1969.

Lowi, T. J. *The politics of disorder.* New York: Basic Books, Inc., 1971.

Luce, R. D., & Raiffa, H. *Games and decisions: Introductions and critical survey.* New York: John Wiley & Sons, 1957.

McClintock, C. G., & McNeil, S. P. Reward and score feedback as determinants of cooperative and competitive behavior. *Journal of Personality and Social Psychology*, 1966, *4*, pp. 606-613.

McClintock, C. G., & McNeel, S. P. Prior dyadic experience and monetary reward as determinants of cooperative and competitive game behavior. *Journal of Personality and Social Psychology*, 1967, *5*, pp. 282-294.

McGregor, D. *The human side of enterprise.* New York: McGraw-Hill, Inc., 1960.

McNeil, K. Understanding organizational power: Building on the Weberian legacy. *Administrative Science Quarterly*, March 1978, *23*, pp. 65-90.

MacPherson, C. B. *Democratic theory: Essays in retrieval.* Oxford: Clarendon Press, 1973.

Machiavelli, N. *The prince and the discourses.* M. Lerner, Ed. New York: Modern Library, 1948.

Madison, J. Federalist 10. *The Federalist papers.* New York: New American Library, 1962.

Madsen, M. C. Cooperative and competitive motivation of children in three Mexican subcultures. *Psychological Reports*, 1967, *20*, pp. 1307-1320.

Madsen, M. C. Developmental and cross-cultural differences in cooperative and competitive behavior of young children. *Journal of Cross-Cultural Psychology*, 1971, *2*, pp. 365-371.

Madsen, M. C., & Connor, C. Cooperative and Competitive behavior of retarded and nonretarded children at two ages. *Child Development*, 1973, *44*, pp. 175-178.

Madsen, M. C., & Shapira, A. Cooperative and competitive behavior of urban Afro-American, Anglo-American, Mexican-American and Mexican village children. *Developmental Psychology*, 1970, *3*, pp. 16-20.

Maller, J. B. *Cooperation and competition.* New York: Teachers College
Press, 1929.

Malthus, T. R. *Essay on the principle of population, 1798, 1803.* New
York: Macmillan, 1894.

Manley, M. *The politics of change: A Jamaican testament.* London:
André Deutsch Limited, 1974.

Marglin, S. What do bosses do?: The origins and functions of hierarchy in
capitalist production. *The Review of Radical Political Economics*,
1974, *6 (2)*, pp. 60-112.

Margolin, J. B. *The effect of perceived cooperation or competition on the
transfer of hostility.* Ph.D. dissertation, New York University, 1954.

Margulies, N., & Wallace, J. *Organizational change: Techniques and applications.* Glenview, Ill.: Scott, Foresman, & Co., 1973.

Martindale, D. *The nature and types of sociological theory.* Boston:
Houghton Mifflin Co., 1960.

Maslow, A. H. The superior person. In W. G. Bennis, Ed., *American
bureaucracy.* Chicago: Aldine (Transaction Books), 1970.

Mead, G. H. *Mind, self and society.* Chicago: University of Chicago Press,
1934.

Melcher, A. J. *Structure and process of organizations: A systems approach.* Englewood Cliffs: Prentice-Hall, Inc., 1976.

Meyer, H. H. The pay-for-performance dilemma. *Organizational Dynamics*, Winter 1975, *3 (3)*, pp. 39-50.

Miles, M. B. On temporary systems. In M. B. Miles, Ed., *Innovation in
education.* New York: Teachers College Press, 1964, pp. 437-490.

Milgram, S. M. *Obedience to authority: An experimental view.* New York:
Harper & Row, 1974.

Miller, A. G., & Thomas, R. Cooperation and competition among Black-
foot Indian and urban Canadian children. *Child Development*, 1972,
43, pp. 1104-1110.

Miller, L., & Hamblin, R. Interdependence, differential rewarding, and
productivity. *American Sociological Review*, 1963, *28*, pp. 768-778.

Mills, C. W. *White collar.* New York: Oxford University Press, 1951.

Mintz, A. Nonadaptive group behavior. *The Journal of Abnormal and
Social Psychology*, 1951, *46*, pp. 150-159.

Mizuhara, T., & Tamai, S. Experimental studies of cooperation and
competition. *Japanese Journal of Psychology*, 1952, *22*, pp. 124-127.

Montagu, A. *The humanization of man.* New York: World Publishing
Co., 1962, p. 297.

Moore, W. E. But some are more equal than others. *American Sociological Review*, 1963, *28 (1)*, pp. 13-18.

Morris, C. W. *Varieties of human value.* Chicago: University of Chicago Press, 1956.

Morrow, A. A., & Thayer, F. C. Collaborative work settings: New titles, old contradictions. In the *Journal of Applied Behavioral Science,* 1977, *13 (3)*, pp. 448-457. Edited by D. G. Appley, D. K. Carew, J. W. Eiseman, F. E. Finch, W. A. Kraus, & A. E. Winder.

Mulder, M. Power equalization through participation? *Administrative Science Quarterly,* 1971, *16 (1)* pp. 31-78.

Myers, A. Team competition, success, and the adjustment of group members. *Journal of Applied and Social Psychology,* 1962, *65,* pp. 325-332.

Napier, R., & Gershenfeld, M. K. *Groups: Theory and experience.* Boston: Houghton Mifflin Co., 1973.

Naught, G. M., & Newman, S. F. The effect of anxiety on motor steadiness in competitive and noncompetitive conditions. *Psychonomic Science,* 1966, *6,* pp. 519-520.

Nelson, L. L. *The development of cooperation and competition in children from ages five to ten years old: Effects of sex situational determinants, and prior experiences.* Ph.D. dissertation, university microfilms, Ann Arbor, Michigan, #71-669, 1970.

Nelson, L., & Kagan, S. Competition: The star-spangled scramble. *Psychology Today,* Sept. 1972, pp. 53-91.

Nichols, J. *Men's liberation: A new definition of masculinity.* New York: Penguin Books, Inc., 1975.

Nielsen, R. P. Stages in moving toward cooperative problem-solving labor relations projects and a case study. *Human Resource Management, 18 (3),* Fall 1979, pp. 2-8.

Niskanen, W. A. *Bureaucracy and representative government.* Chicago: Aldine & Atherton, 1971.

Nixon, R. M. Address to the Nation, Labor Day, 1971.

Notes from the vice-chancellor for student affairs. University of Massachusetts at Amherst, March 1973, *1 (3),* pp. 1-2.

Oates, J. C. New heaven and earth. *Saturday Review,* September 4, 1972, pp. 51-54.

O'Connell, E. J. Effect of cooperative and competitive set on the learning of imitation. *Journal of Experimental Social Psychology,* 1965, *1,* pp. 172-183.

Okun, M. A., & DiVesta, F. J. Cooperation and Competition in co-acting groups. *Journal of Personality and Social Psychology,* 1974, *31 (4),* pp. 615-620.

Orwell, G. *Animal farm.* New York: New American Library of World Literature, Inc., 1946.

Park, R. E., & Burgess, E. W. *Introduction to the science of sociology* (2nd ed.). Chicago: University of Chicago Press, 1924.

Parsons, T. *Structure and process in modern societies.* New York: The Free Press of Glencoe, 1960.

Pateman, C. *Participation and democratic theory.* Cambridge: University Press, 1970.

Patterson, O. Ethnicity and the pluralist fallacy. *Change,* March 1975, 7 (2), pp. 10-11.

Payne, D. Alienation: An organizational-society comparison. *Social Forces,* 1974, *53,* pp. 274-282.

Pfeffer, J. *Organizational design.* Arlington Heights, Ill.: AHM Publishing Corporation, 1978.

Phillips, B. N. *An experimental study of the effects of cooperation and competition, intelligence, and cohesiveness on the task efficiency and process behavior of small groups.* Unpublished Ph.D. dissertation, Indiana University, 1954.

Phillips, B. W., & D'Amico, L. A. Effects of cooperation and competition on the cohesiveness of small face-to-face groups. *Journal of Educational Psychology,* 1956, *47,* pp. 65-70.

Pirsig, R. M. *Zen and the art of motorcycle maintenance.* New York: Bantam Books, Inc., 1974.

Pondy, L. R. Organizational conflict: Concepts and models. *Administrative Science Quarterly,* Sept. 1967, *12,* p. 299.

Presthus, R. Authority in organizations. *Public Administration Review,* Spring 1960, *20* (2).

Presthus, R. *The organizational society,* (revised edition). New York: St. Martin's Press, Inc., 1978.

Raven, B. H., & Eachus, H. T. Cooperation and competition in means-interdependent triads. *Journal of Abnormal Social Psychology,* 1963, *67,* pp. 307-316.

Rawls, J. *A theory of justice.* Cambridge: Belknap Press, 1971.

Read, W. H. Upward communication in industrial hierarchies. *Human Relations,* 1962, *15,* pp. 3-15.

Reich, C. *The greening of America.* New York: Random House, Inc., 1970.

Ricci, D. *Community power and democratic theory: The logic of political analysis.* New York: Random House, 1971.

Roeber, R. J. C. *The organization in a changing environment.* Reading, Mass.: Addison-Wesley, 1973.

Rogers, C. R. Toward a modern approach to values: The valuing process in the mature person. *Journal of Abnormal and Social Psychology,* 1964, *68* (2), pp. 160-167.

Rothschild-Whitt, J. The collectivist organization: An alternative to rational-bureaucratic models. *American Sociological Review*, August, 1979, *44*, pp. 509-527.

Russel, B. *Power: A new social analysis*. London: Allen & Unwin, Ltd. 1938.

Ryan, F. L., & Wheeler, R. *Relative effects of two environments on the way a similation game is played by elementary school students*. Paper presented at the American Educational Research Association meeting, New Orleans, February 26, 1973.

Schermerhorn, J. R. The determinants of cooperative interorganizational relations: Notes toward a working model. *Working paper number 91*, Graduate School of Business Administration, Tulane University, New Orleans, Louisiana, 70118, August, 1973.

Schermerhorn, J. R. Hospital administrator openness to programs of interhospital cooperation. *Working paper Number 93*, Graduate School of Business Administration, Tulane University, New Orleans, Louisiana, 70118, 1974a.

Schermerhorn, J. R. Determinants of interorganizational cooperation. *Working Paper Number 96*, Graduate School of Business Administration, Tulane University, New Orleans, Louisiana, 70118, May, 1974b.

Schumpeter, J. A. *Capitalism, socialism, and democracy* (3rd ed.). New York: Harper & Row, 1950.

Schwartz, T. M. Characteristics of organizational climate and managerial job satisfaction: An empirical study. *Psychology Reports*, Aug. 1975, *37*, pp. 299-305.

Seodel, A., Minas, J. S., Ratoosh, P., & Lipez, M. Some descriptive aspects of two-person non-zero-sum games. *Journal of Conflict Resolution*, 1959, *3*, pp. 114-119.

Scott, W. E., & Cherrington, D. J. The effects of competitive cooperative and individualistic reinforcement contingencies. *The Journal of Personality and Social Psychology*, 1974, *30 (6)*, pp. 748-758.

Scott, W. G. Organization theory: A reassessment. *Academy of Management Journal*, June 1974, *17 (2)*, pp. 242-254.

Scott, W. G., & Mitchell, T. R. *Organization theory: A structural and behavioral analysis*. Homewood, Ill.: Irwin, 1972.

Shapira, A., & Madsen, M. C. Cooperative and competitive behavior of kibbutz and urban children in Israel. *Child Development*, 1969, *40*, pp. 609-617.

Shaw, M. E. Some motivational factors in cooperation and competition. *Journal of Personality*, 1958, *26*, pp. 155-169.

Sherif, M., & Sherif, C. M. *An outline of social psychology*. New York: Harper & Row, 1956.

Sherif, M., Harvey, O. J., White, B. J., Hood, W. R., & Sherif, C. *Intergroup conflict and cooperation: The robbers cave experiment.* Norman, Oklahoma: University Book Exchange, 1961.

Silverman, D. *The theory of organizations.* London: Heinemann, 1970.

Simon, H. A. Authority. In C. M. Arensberg, et al., Eds., *Research in industrial human relations.* New York: Harper & Row, 1957.

Simon, H. A. *Administrative behavior: A study of decision-making processes in administrative organization* (3rd ed.). New York: The Free Press, 1976.

Siu, R. G. H. Work and serenity. *Journal of Occupational Mental Health,* 1971, *1* (*1*), pp. 2-6.

Slater, P. *The pursuit of loneliness: American culture at the breaking point.* Boston: Beacon Press, 1970.

Slater, P. *Earthwalk.* Garden City: Anchor Press, 1974.

Smith, A. *The wealth of nations.* New York: Modern Library, 1937.

Smith, C. G., Ed. *Conflict resolution: Contributions of the behavioral sciences.* Notre Dame: University of Notre Dame Press, 1971.

Smith, A. J., Madden, H. E., & Sobel, R. Productivity and recall in cooperative and competitive discussion groups. *Journal of Psychology,* 1957, *43,* pp. 193-204.

Smith, R. Wider role for worker aired. *The Hartford Courant,* February 22, 1979.

Snider, J. G., & Osgood, C. E., Eds. *Semantiç differential technique.* Chicago: Aldine Publishing Co., 1969.

Staub, E. Helping a person in distress: The influence of implicit and explicit 'rules' of conduct on children and adults. *Journal of Personality and Social Psychology,* 1971, *17,* pp. 137-144.

Steele, F. *Consulting for organizational change.* Amherst: University of Massachusetts Press, 1975.

Stendler, C., Damrin, D., & Haines, A. Studies in cooperation and competition: 1. The effects of working for group and individual rewards on the social climate of children's groups. *Journal of Genetic Psychology,* 1951, *79,* pp. 173-179.

Strauss, G. Tactics of lateral relationships: The purchasing agent. *Administrative Science Quarterly,* 1962, 7, pp. 161-186.

Swingle, P. G. *The management of power.* Hillsdale, N. J.: Lawrence Erlbaum Associates, Inc., 1976.

Swingle, P. G., & Coady, H. Effects of the partner's abrupt strategy change upon subject's responding in the prisoner's dilemma. *Journal of Personality and Social Psychology,* 1967, *5,* pp. 357-363.

Szent-Gyorgyi, A. *The crazy ape.* New York: Philosophical Library, Inc., 1970.

Tannenbaum, A. S., Kavcic, B., Rosner, M., Vianello, M., & Wiesner, G. *Hierarchy in organizations: An international comparison.* San Francisco: Jossey-Bass, 1974.

Tannenbaum, R., & Davis, S. A. Values, man, and organizations. *Industrial Management Review,* 1969, *10* (2), pp. 67-86.

Tarbell, L. *Toward a self-directed community: An exploratory study of alternative groups in the Amherst area.* Unpublished paper, School of Business Administration, University of Massachusetts, Amherst, Mass., August, 1976.

Terkel, S. *Working.* New York: Avon Books, 1975.

Thayer, F. C. *An end to hierarchy! An end to competition! Organizing the politics and economics of survival.* New York: Franklin Watts, Inc., 1973.

Thomas, E. J. Effects of facilitative role interdependence on group functioning. *Human Relations,* 1957, *10,* pp. 347-366.

Thompson, J. D., & McEwen, W. J. Organizational goals and environment: Goal-setting as an interaction process. *American Sociological Review,* 1958, *23,* pp. 23-31.

Thompson, J. D. *Organizations in action.* New York: McGraw-Hill, Inc., 1967.

Thorsrud, E. A strategy for research and social change in industry: A report on the industrial democracy project in Norway. *Social Science Information, 9* (5), pp. 65-90. Paris: Conseil International des Science Sociales, 1970.

Thorsrud, E. Sociological approach to industrial democracy in Norway. In R. Dubin, Ed., *Handbook of work organization and society.* Chicago: Rand McNally, 1976.

Tocqueville, A. *Democracy in America.* Chicago: The Great Books Foundation, 1945. (Great Books Edition published 1955.)

Toffler, A. What is anticipatory democracy? *The Futurist,* Oct. 1975, *9*(5), pp. 224-229.

Toynbee, A. J. *Change and habit: The challenge of our time.* Oxford University Press, 1966.

Triplett, N. The dynamogenic factors in peacemaking and competition. *American Journal of Psychology,* 1897, *9,* pp. 507-533.

Trist, E. Toward a postindustrial culture. In M. Dunnette, Ed., *Handbook of industrial and organizational psychology.* Chicago: Rand McNally, 1976, pp. 1011-1033.

Tuggle, F. D. *Organizational processes.* Arlington Heights, Ill.: AHM Publishing Corporation, 1978.

Tuite, M. Toward a theory of joint decision making. In M. Tuite, R. Chisolm, M. Radnor, Eds., *Interorganizational decision making.* Chicago: Aldine Publishing Co., 1972.

Tullock, G. *Private wants and public means: An economic analysis of the desirable scope of government.* New York: Basic Books, Inc., 1970.

Tumin, M. M. Some principles of stratification: A critical analysis. *American Sociological Review,* Aug. 1953, *18,* pp. 387-394.

Tumin, M. M. On equality. *American Sociological Review,* Feb. 1963, *28 (1),* pp. 19-26.

Uejio, C. K., & Wrightsman, L. S. Ethnic-group differences in the relationship of trusting attitudes to cooperative behavior. *Psychological Reports,* 1967, *20,* pp. 563-571.

United Press International. Professor wages a fight for peace. *The New York Times,* February 18, 1979.

Vaill, P. Reflections on technology. *Social Change,* 1975, *5 (4),* pp. 3-7.

Van Neuman, J., & Morgenstern. *Theory of games and economic behavior.* Princeton, N. J.: Princeton University Press, 1947.

Vickers, Sir G. *Towards a sociology of management.* New York: Basic Books, Inc., 1967.

Vroom, V. H., & Yetton, P. W. *Leadership and decision making.* Pittsburgh: University of Pittsburgh Press, 1973.

Wade, M. The half-time working man. *Vision,* May 1974, pp. 58-62.

Walton, R. E. Two strategies of social change and their dilemmas. *Journal of Applied Behavioral Science,* 1965, *1 (2),* pp. 167-179.

Walton, R. E. *Interpersonal peacemaking: Confrontations and third party consultation.* Reading, Mass.: Addison-Wesley, 1969.

Walton, R. E. How to choose between strategies of conflict and collaboration. In Golembiewski & Blumberg, Eds., *Sensitivity training and the laboratory approach.* Itasca, Ill.: F. L. Peacock, Publishers, 1970, pp. 336-337.

Walton, R. E. Frontiers beckoning the organizational psychologist. *Journal of Applied Behavioral Science,* 1972, *8 (5),* pp. 601-629.

Walton, R. E., & Dutton, J. M. The management of interdepartmental conflict: A model and review. *Administrative Science Quarterly,* 1969, *14,* pp. 73-83.

Wardell, N. N. The corporation. *Daedalus,* Winter 1978, *107 (1),* pp. 97-110.

Warren, R. D., Rogers, D. L. & Evers, F. T. Social system goals in cooperatives. *Rural Sociology,* Spring 1975, *40,* pp. 31-44.

Weber, M. *Essays in Sociology.* H. H. Garth & C. W. Mills, translators. Oxford University Press, 1946.

Weber, M. *The theory of social and economic organizations.* Talcott Parsons, Ed. London: William Hodge, 1947.

Weber, M. Parliament and government in a reconstructed Germany. Appendix 2 to *Economy and society.* New York: Bedminster Press, 1968.

Weick, K. E. *The social psychology of organizing.* Reading, Mass.: Addison-Wesley, 1969.

Weigel, R. H., Wiser, P. L., & Cook, S. W. *The impact of cooperative learning experiences on cross-ethnic relations and attitudes.* Mimeographed report, University of Colorado, Institute of Behavioral Sciences, 1974.

Wheeler, R. C. *A comparison of the effects of cooperative and competitive grouping situations on the perceptions, attitudes, and achievement of elementary school students engaged in social studies inquiry activities.* Unpublished Ph.D. dissertation, University of Minnesota, 1972.

Whisler, T. L. *The impact of computers on organizations.* New York: Praeger Publishers, 1970.

Willis, R. H. & Joseph, M. L. Bargaining behavior. I: "prominence" as a predictor of the outcome of a games agreement. Conflict Resolution, 1959, 3, pp. 102-113.

Wilpert, B. *Codetermination laws in Germany — Externally induced organizational change.* Presented at the International Institute of Management, Berlin, May 1973.

Wilson, W., & Miller, N. Shifts in evaluation of participants following intergroup competition. *Journal of Abnormal and Social Psychology,* 1961, *63*, pp. 428-432.

Woodward, J. *Industrial organization: Theory & practice.* London: Oxford University Press, 1965.

Work in America. Report of a special task force to the secretary of Health, Education and Welfare. Cambridge: M.I.T. Press, 1973.

Workie, A. The effects of cooperation and competition on productivity. Ph.D. dissertation, Teachers College, Columbia University, 1967.

Zajonc, R. B., & Marin, I. C. Cooperation, competition, and interpersonal attitudes in small groups. *Psychonomic Science,* 1967, 7, pp. 271-272.

Zaleznik, A. Power and politics in organizational life. In D. R. Hampton, C. E. Summer, & R. A. Webber. *Organizational behavior and the practice of management.* Glenview, Ill.: Scott, Foresman, 1973.

INDEX